LOVING GOD

HOPE AGU – LITTLE MARY OF THE MOST SACRED HEART OF JESUS

LOVING GOD

Bibliographical Information of the Deutsche Nationalbibliothek
This publication is listed in the Deutsche Nationalbibliographie of the
Deutsche Nationalbibliothek; detailed bibliographical information
can be accessed under http: //dnb.d-nb.de

© 2016 Agu Hope
Printing, Production and Layout: BoD – Books on Demand, Norderstedt
ISBN: 978-3-7431-2980-1

Contents

Preface	7
Introduction	9
I. God's identity	13
II. The Fall	19
III. The Trap	27
IV. Frying pan into fire	34
V. The Awakening	47
VI. The Separation	58
VII. Overcoming	75
VIII. Falling in love	105
IX. Being in love	115
X. My Mum, The Blessed Virgin	136
XI. The Beloved in the Eucharist	146
XII. God the Father	155
XIII. My way of loving God the Father	162
XIV. Conclusion	172

Preface

Considering the universe, Heaven and earth, the Firmament, the creation, one is filled with awe for the Creator whose infinite Wisdom is far beyond human imagination. Regarding the beauty of nature one is overwhelmed at the greatness of the wisdom behind the constructional establishment of such huge phenomenon beyond human comprehension. Then arises suddenly the instinctive inquisitiveness, the urge of seeking answers and explanations to satisfy the uneasiness of the human mind. Whereby the inability and the inadequacy of the human mind in its limitations to contemplate the source of such great magnificence that only God can bring into existence, gives rise to wonder, consequently culminating in notions of doubt, creating an impregnable mind that gives birth to belief in nature rather than in the Creator who is God and so atheism is born. Nonetheless, the creation itself, nature, in its entirety speaks of the existence of God who is found in His creation and in man himself. The beauty of creation radiates the wisdom, the magnificence and the beauty of the Creator. The lack of comprehension of the great wisdom behind the creation that calls for the denial of the existence of God, as atheists do, does not rule out the existence of God, for man is a sure proof of the existence of God being himself a created being and a wonder.

The tendency of man, in his conceit, to believe in nature rather than in the Creator, God, to diverge from reality to atheism, ignoring the God given intellect and reason by which He is clearly portrayed in His wonderful, beautiful, magnificent creation, is inexcusable, for this pitiable state is a product of self exultation and conceit. The denial of the existence of God is a tragedy, a heresy, ingratitude, inexcusable and uncalled for attitude towards a very loving, kind, patient, good and tender loving God Who sacrificed all that is dear to Him, His only begotten Son, for the love and good of Humanity. O man, awake from slumber and recognize your Father in Heaven, He is God! To turn the back to Him, to give Him a denial and a deaf ear, despite all the evidence leading to His existence, meant to capture the attention of every level-headed human being endowed with reason by His Creator, that He is, paves way to perdition.

"Loving God" is a personal encounter with the living God, intended to throw some light to the minds of the doubtful, enhance the beauty of the hearts docile to God's Love and radiate the sweetness in loving and being loved by God.

Introduction

In September 1949 a bouncing baby girl was born to a humble couple Matthew and Flora Agu in Enugu the capital of the then eastern Nigeria, Christians of the Anglican faith. A daughter they dote on, so much so it appeared they would grant her anything for the asking, even carrying water from Enugu, to her at school, in her second year at St. Catherine's girl's secondary school Nkwere, Orlu, a boarding school almost about a hundred miles distance from their residence, merely because she complained the water in her school was not fit for drinking. It's amazing how they coped with it all each time she came up with something new in her attempts for attention, pretending sick or threats to end her life if they failed to show up during their parents day or during any special festivities. Perhaps, one may try to understand them having lost their first child, a baby boy, therefore, their next child became everything, a consolation to their aching hearts. A child who gave profound peace to Flora. This child they baptized and gave the name Hope.

The eldest of six children, two boys and four girls. Her father, a Treasurer in the municipal council, local government Enugu, a man of substantial income who could afford a comfortable living for his family, was a devout and practical Christian. His life-style was – Godliness with contentment is great gain – and this mode of life he imparted to his children and so imbedded the fear of God in them. An honest man who would have swimmed in wealth, had that been his objective, as he had ample opportunities to acquire worldly riches, but realized transient is the smile of such enrichment therefore, he made provision in Heaven, hence the mortal body decays after one expires, but the soul lives eternally in Heaven or in Hell, the acquired riches left behind. Heaven and Hell are two respective realities. Doubting the reality of these established facts does not extinguish their existence. Anyone who doubts the existence of hell will find out when he gets there, unfortunately though, there would not be any possibility of turning back as the die would then be cast. Nevertheless, each individual is responsible for the final destination of his soul after expiration.

However, in the course of time, in their quest to worship God in a more reverenced and authentic manner, rather than in superfluous and flamboyant display of materialism they deviated from Anglican church, ignorantly, to a sectarian church – Christ Apostolic church – which almost ruined the life of Hope had Providence not intervened. Hope, a disciplined and well brought up girl, whose parents dote on, schooled in a private school, a boarding school, Zixton primary school Ozobulu, the best private school at the time in the region of their habitat, attended also one of the best secondary schools of the region, St. Catherine's girls secondary school Nkwere, known for the best performance of the students in west African school certificate examinations, excelling always with flying colors, became a prey for the instruments of Satan under the camouflage of messengers of God.

This was the aftermath of the horrible Nigerian civil war with its end in early 1970 which paved way for Satan, the enemy of God and humanity, to manifest his falsehood by feeding the so called prophets of the apostolic church with lies concerning Hope. It was the will of God she should marry a Nigerian diplomat in Washington D.C they told her parents, a total stranger, unknown to them, manipulating the mind of her father who was filled with the fear of God. Consequently, in sept. 1971 Hope, who lived a protected life, left the four walls of her parental home into the unknown and began to go through many waters. The door to the inevitable was thrown open and the forces of darkness began to have their feed, aiming at destroying the faith of her father who stood firm, despite the storm, having built his house on the Rock. Hope's consolation in all the turmoil was her father's acceptance of the catholic faith, the One Holy, Catholic and Apostolic Church founded by Jesus Christ just before his departure from this life and so turned his back to the apostolic church and all the so called Pentecostal churches. It is essential for every Christian to realize, all that glitters is not gold therefore, look properly before leaping.

I. God's identity

It is a wonder and amazingly interesting the realization nothing existed at the beginning except God. There was no Heaven, no Angels, no earth, the Firmament, birds, oceans, human beings, mountains animals and so on, absolutely nothing except God. Then in His leisure, for His pleasure, He began to create. He created Heaven and the Angels and all that is in it. He created the Firmament and the earth and all in it. Of all His creation He fell in love with man, Adam, to whom He gave everything He could possibly give for his comfort as He created him in His own image, and kept him in the Garden of Eden where he lacked nothing. God loved Adam so much as to leave him with his free-will expecting His love for him to be reciprocated. Adam endowed with so many Graces and Virtues such as sincerity, immortality, free from suffering and pain and the possession of natural and supernatural life. He was a child and friend of God created to be lavished with love and affection. For the perfection of his comfort God created for him, from his rib, while he slept, a companion, Eve, with whom he could not resist the enticement of Satan. The inability to detect the craftiness of Satan, the greed to become like God gave rise to the betrayal of a most loving and wonderful God in deepest consequence. Thus man failed woefully and disappointed God. Man began to taste pain and suffering, insincere, and immoral. He became sinful. Therefore, God was displeased and drove him out from the Garden of Eden. His displeasure extended to their descendants from generation upon generation. Adam was left with no alternative but death as inheritance for his descendants.

Love is not just a word, it is Divine, it is God. "Love is patient and kind; Love is not jealous or boastful; it is not arrogant or rude. Love does not insist on its own way; it is not irritable or resentful; it does not rejoice at wrong, but rejoices in the right. Love bears all things, believes all things, hopes all things, endures all things. Love never ends,, Therefore, God being Love and unable to bear the separation, the distance between Him and His disobedient children, chose a nation to model after His own nature, in order to see His reflection in them and derive pleasure in being a Father. A nation as a model for other nations. It is His desire to share His Divine life with His Children. In this way the Father Children relationship would be reinstated. But this vision of God was nothing but far-fetched. O how His Heart yearned for the love of His children who sought Him only in time of need to dive into disobedience in time of plenty and comfort. All they could offer a loving and tender caring Father was lip service. Once again man failed God and His Heart was devastated. God was suffering. Love was suffering. But for reasons beyond human comprehension, this God who is Almighty, the great I AM, Author and Giver of Life, being madly in love with man, would stop at nothing to win back the love of His children and set them free from the deadly poison of sin, from the power of darkness.

Therefore, at the fullness of time He became "flesh and dwelt among us,, a final attempt to win back the love of His children and save them from damnation programmed by the fall of Adam and Eve their first parents. "In the beginning was the Word and the Word was with God and the Word was God,, It was time for the salvation of man. The long expected Messiah, foretold in the pages of the Old Testament by the prophets, in the psalms, was to become flesh in the womb of a Virgin. This popular miraculous event of the incarnation began with the annunciation of the Archangel Gabriel to Mary, a virgin, betrothed to Joseph, of the house of David, a carpenter by profession. It is interesting to note the Almighty God chose a poor humble Virgin to be His mother and a humble Carpenter to be His Guardian. How amazing, the Creator of the Universe, the Author and Giver of Life, chose to dwell among men, and be born of poor humble parents, in a stable, wrapped in a swaddling cloth and laid in a manger. The fascination of it all, He did not only choose a life of poverty, there was no place for Him and His parents at the Inn for His Mother to give birth, whereas everything both in Heaven and on Earth belongs to Him. In Heaven the Angels worship and adore Him. The Cherubim and Seraphin prostrate before Him. Why would God choose poverty instead of being adorned with the riches of this world, His own right. His earthly mission was of redemptive motivation, therefore, intended to underline the perishable nature of worldly possessions. It is more beneficial and safe for man to acquire wealth in Heaven, which is everlasting and secure, rather than be dependent on worldly possession whose fate is transient. To this end He began His ministry at the age of thirty, having survived a hazardous childhood whereby His life was threatened and was compelled to go into exile with His parents to Egypt. In the attempt to reach Him King Herod, fearing a threat to his kingly position, became responsible for the death of several innocent children under the age of two.

However, Jesus, the long expected Messiah, God incarnate, proclaimed the coming of the kingdom of God and called for conversion and forgave the sins of those who approached Him in humble trust. He healed the sick, the lame walked, the dead rose, the blind saw and so many other miracles He performed. He became popular. Crowds thronged to be relieved of their ailments, but that was it. Although some took Him to be a great prophet, for no one ever spoke with authority or performed the miraculous things He performed, He was never really understood, not even His twelve Apostles who witnessed His supernatural powers such as walking on water, calming the storm "who is this that even the winds obey Him" and His transfiguration on mount Tabor when the Glory of God shone on His Face like the sun while His Garment was white as light, and Moses and Elijah spoke with Him. How sad, one who had so much love and compassion to give was rejected. He came unto His own and His own received Him not. God was lonely on Earth, very lonely in the midst of His own. God was rejected by His own creatures. In His own town Nazareth, He was just the carpenter's son, to others a nuisance merely interfering with the affairs of the Scribes and Pharisees, hence the messiah was to be of a kingly family not a pauper, which consequently led to His denouncement by the Sanhedrin and His ultimate deliverance to Pilate, the Roman proconsul, who condemned Him to death by crucifixion.

Now the time was ticking for a programmed conspiracy against the innocent Lamb of God by the Rabbis, teachers of the synagogue who saw Jesus as being thwarted in their ambitious aspirations as the leaders of the people. Greed is a flaw in character, when it germinates, it produces selfishness, blindness, arrogance, and deafness to sound reasoning. With the maturity of this conspiracy the Rabbis, to reach Jesus and silence Him, sought the assistance of a very close friend of His, one of His Apostles, Judas, who did not hesitate to sell friendship for thirty pieces of silver, thereby betraying someone who trusted him, a man who shared the secret of his life with him. A man he ate with from the same plate. Blinded by Greed he betrayed his best friend with a kiss. Could anything be more apathetic, more disappointing, and more ignoble than to spit at friendship on the face. This betrayal on the part of Judas paved way to the incredible torment Jesus was to undergo. What a world poor Jesus had to face, even the taste of a true friendship was denied Him. A very lonely Man he was, in the cloak of humanity, who was neither understood nor was anyone His standard, always the compassionate Giver, who shared and understood every problem of those around Him.

Jesus, who during His three years of public life taught openly in the synagogues, showered compassion on all and healed their ailments was now at the mercy of the Sanhedrin who delightfully delivered Him, their brother, into the Hands of the Romans, who were for them the "gentiles", with false accusations. His words were twisted and taken out of context. The hour of darkness has begun. Love was on trial. Jesus was unjustly tried and condemned to death by crucifixion on the cross which during His time was a capital punishment, a symbol of ignominy and failure.

The choice of a murderer, a robber, to the Son of Man, an innocent and righteous Man, Jesus Christ, the God Man reveals the depth of the effect of sin man inherited from Adam and Eve. It unveiled the nature of Satan the father of lies and evil. In Satan's vocabulary there is nothing like goodness or sympathy. Therefore, his time was come, the hour of darkness, he manipulated and instigated God's children against God to have God be crucified on the cross with the worse torture and humiliation ever possible, aiming at breaking Him down in order to consequently make His redemptive mission a failure. Could anything be more disappointingly heart-rending to a God of Love than to observe wickedness in her complete nakedness, engulf humanity, His own Creatures, His Beloved Children, to portray herself in her worse shape to bury true human feelings in the sea of evil. But God would not be broken. He would not give up. There was too much at stake. He would not live without His children. Oh! How He was tortured. What an irony, the torturers took their own Father, their Savior, for their enemy, made Him a prey for their sadistic pleasure, instigated by Satan, their real enemy, against a friend, against their flesh and blood, their Heavenly Father. Nevertheless, in His goodness and love He forgave His enemies "Father forgive them for they know not what they do,, and after three hours of hanging on the cross, under the weight of His body, He breathed his last. Love was crucified, Love died. Cardinal Newman said, "the cross of our dear Savior has set a new value upon all the hopes, all the rivalries, all achievements of mortal man. It is the melody into which all the tunes of music of this world are utterly to revolve." Fortunately the triumphant resurrection of our dear Lord and Savior defeated death, and worn eternal Life for man. Now man has a right to live, on the condition he returns love for love. He has to accept God's love and love God in return.

Consequent to the mess Adam and Eve made in subjecting themselves to the mischievousness of Satan which led to their betrayal of the God of love, Who beautifully and richly adorned them with Graces whereby they lacked nothing, with their ignoble act of disobedience, desiring to be like God, they fell woefully in His sight and disappointed Him. On the other hand, having created man in his own image, man being part of God, the crown of His Creation, to whom He gave His Heart and wishes him to share in His Divine Life, in order to restore man to his original glory and reconcile him to Himself God came down and lived in this world stained by sin, tasting every pain of mind, soul, spirit and body more than we will ever know. He was never fully understood by anyone and one can imagine the pain of not being understood by ones own. He was treated as though He was the worse criminal that ever lived, stripped of every respect, scourged, mocked, spat at on the face, slapped, crowned with thorns, pulled like a beast of burden, humiliated, stripped publicly before a sea of people and nailed on the cross. The good Lord bore all in silence. He was left hanging on the cross for three good hours to die with a broken heart under the weight of His Body. O man! how long would you remain in slumber, how long would you be blind, how long would you lack compassion, how long would you keep the door of your heart locked up against the God Who created you ? O, if only you knew what it would be like spending eternity with Satan in hell you would do anything possible, while you can, to choose Eternal life in Heaven which God lovingly offers you in Jesus Christ, for Him and With Him. It is wisdom to give the heart to God for this means eternal Life for you unless you desire, on your own free-will, eternal death.

II. The Fall

During my second grade in the secondary school, at St. Catherine's girls secondary school Nkwere in Orlu local government in the then eastern Nigeria, I had a sophisticated London trained teacher, Mrs. Ohiaeri, fair in complexion, of average height, slightly plump with a cheerful disposition. I can well remember the impression her statement "chastity is like a crown on the wearer's head" made on me. If that was naive, I would not know, but I vowed to myself it would be my wedding gift to whoever I would decide to spend my life with in the future. I was very comfortable with this decision and chastity being like a crown on the wearer's head became my moto. This was a time when it was "in,, to have boyfriends and those without were said to be "out,,. Little did that disturb me, being raised up in a good Christian home, I had my vision before me and was determined to achieve it.

With my average height, I was favored with a fair complexion, a pretty face, well proportioned physical attribute, and a friendly disposition. As a girl who hardly got annoyed, if at all, melts at the smile of the offender and always ready to apologize should I offend anyone. Somehow, I got to apologizing sometimes even when I was offended. In other words, saying "I am sorry,, never was a big deal to me. It seemed quite natural and genuine. I was equally gifted to sharing and always had the least of what ever I had to eat, after sharing among those in my company, without bothering. I was a girl who could easily make friends and I had a handful of them, most of them from wealthy families. Just as would be expected I had hobbies like everyone else. My hobbies were teaching Sunday school children, reading, cooking, writing stories, acting, instructing and organizing play groups. Being interested in literature I was in the literary society at school, debating society, choral society, although I wouldn't consider myself talented in singing, but just for the fun of it, and in Dramatic society which I found exciting and participated in several plays. I was quite a happy girl with a bright future, until the inevitable happened, the formidable Nigerian civil war was ushered in and nothing was the same again.

Not long after the surge of the war did it began to show it's ugliest face. People were forced to abandon their habitat to strange places with little or nothing. Poverty became the order of the day and moral decay rose to it's highest peak. The flashy colorful uniform of the military soon captured the fancy of young girls and teenage girls in particular, posing a threat to their character formation, being unable to resist the allure of the gallantry of the men who wore them, as education came to a standstill and boredom was born. The military on their part, did not hesitate to take advantage of the situation. My parents however, were able to shield me and my sisters from being their prey and so we could eschew ourselves from such evil enticement, the handwriting of Satan. The family occupied herself with regular attendance of church services, thereby placing us children in constant awareness of the presence of God.

Nevertheless, one cannot stop the inevitable. The on raging war instigated a state of agitation on the minds of the youth. Everyone wanted to be useful to the nation as rumor had it those who assisted the nation one way or the other would be compensated by the government in a special way. This being the situation I organized a play group called "The rising sun play group" with girls only, for the purpose of raising fund for the war. Unexpectedly, the play group was a success and became the talk of the town. We were able to put up a good performance of the "Barrettes of Wimpole Street" which captured the fancy and appreciation of the European expatriates working with the caritas, a catholic relief organization. The play group enjoyed the assistance of the parish priest who offered her the school hall and every other help needed, during practice that enabled her to achieve the admiration she won with the performance.

Trouble never blows a whistle they say, and all that glitters is not gold. With the success of the play group came dinner invitations from the priest which we usually, without hesitation, accepted. At the end of each dinner, relief materials, such as food, clothes and blankets were offered to the girls. This was possible due to the access of the priest, a handsome young man in his middle thirties, fair in complexion, and of good disposition, to the area relief materials, from the catholic relief organization, caritas, stored in his parish. In the course of time the invitations no longer was collectively, but rather individually. The invitations, an avenue of escape from lack and malnutrition was rather an enticing temptation to reject as it provided an asset to good nourishment and relief materials, following the scarcity of essential food items and the lack of means to purchase them in the heat of the war. The attendance of these dinners met with no disapproval on the part of our parents hence they were dinner invitations from a servant of God and they were also well aware of his assistance to our play group. Sometimes we would dine with two or three other priests with him. It was a privilege to be invited to such dinners which presented the opportunity of a better life despite the war. Little did we realize we would have to pay bitterly for such dinners, a means projected to create a confidential and a homely atmosphere that would enable the wolf to strike the prey.

One can imagine me, a well-protected girl of about 19 years old, in the flower of her youth, full of dreams for the future, an innocent girl, the hope of her parents, an insurance for old age, was betrayed by a priest. His amorous advances and sweet words, culminated in infatuation, camouflaged herself in the cloak of love and weakened the resistance of a strong willed girl to a priest of God who would not grant her peace until he disvirgined her. A very sad story that threw the veil of darkness into my life and made me go through many waters. Although I was not catholic then, he had no right to be an instrument of darkness to me. Here was an ordained priest of God whose duty was to protect the children of God but he chose to devour them. Sadly enough, shortly after this episode, the horrible three years civil war came to an abrupt end and we returned to Enugu were we had our residence before the civil war. Perhaps it might be interesting to know the priest managed to locate our residential address in Enugu, which was for me very disgraceful, wondering what in heaven's name came over him to dare to come to my parental home after the pain he caused them, dressed as a catholic priest. What would a catholic priest be doing in a neighborhood of none Catholics. It never rains but it purrs, the priest knelt down before me asking for my hand in marriage and I turned him down. However, he later gave up his priesthood and got married to some other girl. When my mother heard he intended to marry me her answer was simple and straight "My daughter will never marry a fallen-away man of God"

It is rather sad some priests forget they are open letters and ambassadors of Christ. When they consecrate themselves to Jesus Christ they should live up to their vows. If only these priests would realize the privilege they have to represent Christ, so to say be another Christ, they would seek God's Grace to put flesh under subjection like St. Paul did. They would always start their day with the blessing of the God they serve by observing Holy Hours early in the morning before the Blessed Sacrament. Any priest who entertains doubt about the real presence of God in the Blessed Sacrament is making the mistake of his life because Jesus is truly present, Body Blood Soul and Divinity in the Blessed Sacrament. For a priest to be a passionate priest he must develope a personal relationship with Jesus and not take Him for granted, He loves us madly, that would be a very big mistake, not only by the priest, but also by every Christian. He is Love, yes, He wants also His love to be reciprocated. He desires to see the reflection of Himself in His children. It is most irritating and sad that those few priests who are weak and fail to put flesh under subjection soil the names of faithful and passionate ones. There is no temptation one cannot be able to overcome for God is faithful and will not allow us to be tempted above that which we are able. Everything lies in the mind. If only one would have a strong will coupled with prayer there is nothing one cannot overcome trusting in God. These weak priests have the full knowledge of the truth therefore, they should not give room to the enemy, the Satan, who would not stop at nothing to seduce the children of God. It would be a grievous error to take God's Grace for granted. Whoever shall cause these little ones go astray, "it is better that a mill stone be hung on his neck and he be cast into the sea."

Having been made a scape goat, as the eldest daughter, of by the sectarian church my parents belonged to I was made to travel to the United States of America to be joined to a Nigerian diplomat in Washington. A very sad and ugly event that should never have happened considering the religious status of my parents and the upbringing given to me. My dad an educated and enlightened man who attended the best Grammar school in the state, an Ibadan university graduate, a very humble and God fearing man who would, otherwise, not have succumbed to such a proposal for his elder daughter, well beloved, to travel to a foreign country to marry someone he never knew, had the prophets of the Christ Apostolic Church not told him it was God's will. To feed their greed they perpetrated His faithfulness and loyalty to God into a crime of selfishness, depending on the proposal as an asset to bring in a greater tithe. This being the disclosure of another prophet in a lame attempt to rectify the damage done to me after the die was cast.

In retrospect I felt a great relief no marriage was contracted, although this was not the wish of the diplomat who brought me to Washington to become his bride. As a young girl I had dreams of my Romeo, my prince charming, to my utter disappointment and confusion, on arrival to Washington, I was confronted with a man almost triple my age who could be my father, a divorcee with seven children. One can simply imagine what a shock it all was for a young girl of my caliber. It was like a nightmare and immediately I began agitating to be sent back to my parents and took the initiative to inform them of my dilemma. This would have yielded fruit, as my parents felt concerned and informed him of my plight. There was nothing possible my parents would not do for my happiness because they dote on me. But the man being a diplomat, double-crossed me, and manipulated the minds of my parents with his sweet worded letter, portraying his readiness to give me all the respect, love and care accorded to a married woman, giving them the assurance of me completing my education. My parents unable to recognize the wolf in sheep clothing, having been blinded by their belief the whole affair was God's Will, gave in and my father replied wondering why I was undermining God's choice. I lost every trump. I neither wanted to hurt the feelings of my parents nor did I want to reject God's choice as I did not want to stand alone should my future choice be worse than the so called "God's choice." Little did they know the man was anything but a Christian. Had it been known he was in a secret society, which was a later discovery on my part, my parents would have set everything in motion for my quick return. Unfortunately, by the time this was known I had already stepped into the ring and the die was cast.

Nevertheless, my parents, having made a white wedding essential for their consent, the diplomat had a hard nut to crack. Now, how could a man who already had a white wedding go in for a second one. That was impossible, but the demand of my parents must be met otherwise, he would have had to call the whole show off, which would have been to my favor, instead he chose the game of camouflage and played deceit, much to my disgust. To this end I was led to a boutique where a wedding gown was hired in which some snapshots were made of me wearing it and both of us as wedded couples. A mean display of deceit played on innocent citizens who wouldn't dare hurt the hair of an enemy. For their satisfaction and blessing for a camouflaged marriage, the deceitful wedding photos were sent to them.

I wouldn't say I was naive, or maybe I was, but there was nothing I could have done dealing with a man who had a world of experience, who, knowing fully well my unsuspicious mind, played trick on me, reached out for my travelling documents which he kept in his possession making it difficult for any attempt on my part to desert him.

Nevertheless, this union as it seemed, spelt separation from the very beginning having been built on shifting sand.

In the course of time he was transferred from Washington to Hamburg where he became the consul general of the consulate general. A position which would have been attractive and enchanting to a young girl being the wife of a consul general had the situation been otherwise and I had my prince charming at my side, as it all entailed representation and being in high society. Somehow, the whole affair was nauseating to me and to be seen on the side of a man who could be my father was an unbearable burden. I missed the four walls of my parental home. on one occasion, almost in the ninth month of my unfortunate pregnancy, after launching a ship for my country, during the reception I could no longer bear the deceit of being what I was not anymore and the mask of superficiality beneath the gesture of friendliness in the high society was like a thorn in the flesh and I deserted the scene only to be brought home by the police having lost my way in the darkness of the night. This instigated my ultimate escape from the relationship which was a prison a year after my little girl was born.

Having escaped this ordeal I realized, to my utter dismay, it never rains but it purrs. In my eagerness to put the broken pieces of my life together I saw the necessity to return to Germany. Now a mother, without losing my figure, still attractive and with the objective of completing my studies, I made my way back to Germany, having received the blessing of my parents and also the support of the superintendent of the Apostolic church who prophesied another suitor was waiting for me there. Surprisingly my parents did not learn their lesson. I later realized, God actually knows those who seek to serve Him sincerely and He never fails to draw them to Himself at the right time even though they belong to the wrong denomination or sect. Believing they were actually receiving true messages from God, my parents, were content with the lame excuse of their church, the right suitor was overlooked having been in a haste to accept the first offer and so everything was blamed on the effect of the civil war.

III. The Trap

In summer 1974 I flew back to Hamburg having procured myself with a visa under the privilege of being the wife of the consul general of Nigeria, which I actually wasn't considering the nature of events that led to it. Besides, it lacked the flavor of excitement supposed to accompany such a status, thereby making it tasteless. However, not long after, the inevitable happened and before I knew it I fell from frying pan into fire. The whole sequence of the evil which took place in my life was woven by Satan through his agents to reach my father who was a very humble and faithful servant of God. One needed to know him to be able to understand what I mean. When one gives himself entirely to God then one is faced with the confrontation of Satan in different forms. The consolation thereof is God's continual presence with His beloved, paving way, despite all the storms, for a safe harbor for God never allows anyone to be tempted above his ability. He is always faithful and He never disappoints anyone who puts His trust in Him, so is our Heavenly Father.

There is nothing God loves more than humility and the enemy opposes all that God loves and always comes in the way. So outstanding was the humility of my father it could not escape the comment of one of my sisters husbands "your father is humility itself". The only thing wanting in his life was not being in the one holy catholic and apostolic church founded by Jesus but the grace was granted him just before he expired to be with his Beloved Savior at the age of 91. He lived a fulfilled life despite all the obstacles thrown on his path by our salvations enemy to which the Lord granted him the Grace to overcome. We will not be tempted above that we are able the Scripture tells us and temptations lead to spiritual maturity if only one focuses his attention on Jesus for His Grace is always sufficient. To break the will and confidence of my father in the Almighty God Satan threw the priest on my way and paved way to my being involved with the diplomat making me an unmarried daughter with a child which was the least my father expected of me being his eldest child and well beloved. As though that wasn't enough he placed yet a more devastating obstacle to my happiness that was meant to bring the ultimate ruin of my life and break the back bone of my father.

As Shakespeare rightly put it "the instrument of darkness tell us truth, win us with honest trifles to betray in deepest consequence" Satan is very crafty and can stop at nothing to see to the downfall of the children of God. For seeds to germinate there must be fertile soil, so to this aim Satan chooses mostly those who have fallen from God's Grace, provides the manure by presenting what is not as what is. Satan is actually operating with agents in disguise as angels of light. Unaware of the danger before me, searching for a one room apartment or a furnished room after returning back to Hamburg, the newspaper, the Welt, which usually does not advertise estate agencies or agents on Wednesdays, happened to have mysteriously only one estate agent advertised. The news-vendor, with the aim of doing me a favor, wrote out the address of the estate agent, saving me the waste of money buying the whole paper which was no use to me. The saying is true, one cannot prevent the inevitable. In searching for the estate agent I found myself in an uninviting, hungry looking estate office, after a long search in a lonely street. Scared out of my life, deliberating on turning back, my legs carried me to the office door, I found myself reluctantly knocking on the door, not wanting to go back without giving it a try, having taken such pain to locate the place. To my utter surprise an elderly man, plump, tall, in his middle seventies, shabbily dressed, looking out of his eye glasses, hanging on the tip of his nose as though it would drop to the floor the next instance, ushered me in. With difficulties I managed to hide my fears and informed him of my plight. I was then informed he had no apartment to offer me, "but there is a Nigerian guy who has a furnished room to let." I was cajoled into accepting this furnished room despite my allusion to my resentment to living with a man together in his apartment. Nevertheless, when I finally got to this guy and saw "Bless me oh God" on his door I felt my parents prayer was answered being brought to someone who loves God.

Having moved into this apartment, to my utter bewilderment and amazement I discovered with deep sorrow "Bless me oh God" was a mere camouflage. Everything was planned and arranged by the guy, Anthony, and the evil spirits he served. Few days after I moved into his apartment the horror began to unfold. It gradually dawned on me the grievous mistake I made accepting the offer to live with this guy under the same roof. To have me tied to his evil practices he first disclosed to me his power of prayer, which I never knew such things existed. That one could have contact with God in such form as to write Him a letter on a plain sheet of paper, fold it, murmur something over it and at the same time moving the fingers over it as though it was being sprinkled with water and receive instant reply on the same paper, was a revelation to me. Before I could know it I was maneuvered to believe it was God's will to marry him, according to the message in one of those letters. Having been raised up with the fear of God, believing my parent's prayers brought me there, to a man of God, I gave in, merely due to the fear of God as I was not in love with him. He was not my type and my heart never reached out to him. From this experience, I realized marital union could be harmonious if at least one partner nurtures the fear of God, provided the other one is not an agent of the devil, because only then would it be impossible to please him hence Satan does not believe in Goodness. As I began to realize the awkwardness of the whole situation, unable to please him, failure to observe Christian principles in him, hours of talking on end settling irrelevant matters, being always right, according to him he was to teach me what love is, although I saw no love in him, I realized it was not for me to have happiness in this world therefore, looking out into space through the window one day, I appealed to God to grant me happiness in Heaven. Thereafter, we moved into another apartment when climbing the steps to the apartment became a burden due to pregnancy. From this apartment we moved again into a bigger one for the birth of my second son to enable my children have a room to themselves.

Scary enough, Anthony began, in this apartment, to work, not only with his mysterious letters, but also with the evil spirits he served as they began to manifest. The apartment began to be hunted by evil spirits who left their signature on mirrors with imprints of skeleton fingerprints that spoke of their visit. It was a life of insecurity and uncertainty. Fear, an uninvited guest, and a pest, became a thorn in the flesh, without remedy. The presence of Anthony became to me a guarantee for security, but to my utter dismay the deprivation of his presence was a frequent company, as his hobby was gambling. I felt pity for my children who had no childhood but fear and confusion. I was bullied and scourged with electric cable, spat at, termed stupid. My children were often told their mother was foolish. I had to bear a lot of humiliation before his guests and every woman we happened to know was better than me.

Once I told him he had no respect for me he retorted "I cannot respect you" For him a woman is a slave not a companion. Strange though, I found his character unchristian and without hesitation made it clear to him, but he always shoved it off, yet I stuck to him due to the prayer. All my efforts to be a good Christian wife was not appreciated. When I challenged him of not being a Christian husband, he put it off saying he was teaching me something and only when I learnt it would he change. From his prayer I was asked not to tell him he did not love me and he was to teach me what love is. I was a sinful woman, I was told, therefore, unworthy to give the children lessons on morality. To teach any one about God one must first be clean and for me to be clean penance was necessary. This penance was to get him girls. Moreover, for me to be free from the Nigerian diplomat who was in the secret society to avoid his evil influence, he was the cause of all the problems we encountered, I was told, he was against me having a healthy relationship, I was to bring men to the house who were filmed, from the adjoining room, a store room, while they were on me, through the hole he bore on the wall. To make matters worse I dare not go to church for confession as he was my confessor. In fact I stopped going to mass, according to him, there was no use attending mass as we quarreled much, the quarrels which were usually said to be my fault. Never before did I come across someone very difficult to please, someone who was always right. It is said a tree cannot make a forest and it takes two to make a quarrel, but for him he was faultless. How could one contend with someone who would stand at the gate of heaven ushering people in. A man who never cared about the feelings of others and would stop at nothing provided his aims were achieved, with a very sharp tongue and could easily tell one off with very insulting words, murdering the feelings of his prey without remorse.

I must have been indeed naive to have taken Anthony for a prophet, but what else could I have done when he presented himself as such and was able to tell me correctly about my late step grandmother and knew how she was called. I was strictly instructed not to mention his power of prayer, as he called it, to any one, otherwise I would go insane. The fear of going insane kept me silent. The fear of God, having been instilled in me from childhood, instigated me to attribute it all as my cross and I suffered in silence. My happiness was gone and all my hopes were thrown into the trash. That he did not join me to his secret society was due to the education my parents gave me. My father taught me to think, making it difficult for me to agree to everything he said without first expressing my opinion, which usually ended up in a row as I was expected to accept everything without questioning. According to him, God would correct his error, if at all he had one, to be right. The inability to accept everything without questioning, despite my efforts to do so in order to avoid his long sermon on my foolishness and the lack of the wit to be a good and subordinated wife, saved me from being initiated into his occultism due to our differences.

Despite my unhappiness over the mess with my life, I did try, to no avail, to make a relationship that was doomed from the start to break down to work. Divorce was then a strange word to me, although a frequent allusion by Anthony to boost his ego as the man of the house. The constant boasting he could easily get rid of me for another woman at will, was reason enough for me, under normal circumstances to pack my bag and baggage, but I couldn't. On the long run I ended up apologizing for every quarrel. My concern was my innocent children who were sadistically chastised with handcuffs and scourging with electric cable. One day my elder son, Emmanuel, surprised me with the question "mum, why did you get us such a father? Never mind I will protect you when I grow up, now if I intervened he will scourge me" I was almost reduced to tears. Again, the poor child asked me confidently, feeling concerned, "Papa doesn't take his birth, how can you tolerate that?" It was then I knew God gave me intelligent and observant children who love me despite all the attempts on the part of Anthony to paint me black and foolish before them. The realization of the unhappiness of my children and my inability to help them, added to my distress. Had it not been the fears of madness and offending God, which made me his hostage, I would have said good-bye to it all, taken my children and called it quit. I had such a happy childhood and gave a counterfeit to my poor innocent children. It hurt badly.

On one occasion, to make up for Anthony's negligence of me, for his lack of compliments, and also to make up for the torture I was subjected to under his tongue, which was sharper than razor, Emmanuel ordered, impulsively, through the commercial advertisement on television, some gold jewel, although he knew he would not be able to pay for it, only to watch Anthony angrily send it back to the dealer. Somehow, deep down in his childish heart he had secretly hoped Anthony would pay for it on arrival. One can simply imagine how disappointed the poor child must have been after he was harshly reprimanded for spending a good thought for his poor mother. That my children and I did not go insane was due to God's mercy. There was nothing he did not do to break our back bone, but God in His infinite Mercy, sinful though we be, never forgets His children and when one thinks every door is closed, somehow He opens the window.

Of course I knew people could dream dreams, see vision and prophesy, but the kind of prayer he made was indeed new to me. How could one write questions on a blank type-writer sheet of paper, fold it, tie it with a white thread, murmur something and flank the fingers over it and receive answers written on it, some in cipher, which he alone can interpret, and some in red. One can easily imagine how eerie it all was to me. To make it more eerie, to my utter surprise, my late step grandmother was called exactly by the name she was called when she was alive. How could he have known about her I wondered. I neither mentioned her to him nor did I have any letter from any relation who wrote about her. It was a very big puzzle to me. Hardly did I recover from that did he throw another bombshell namely, I should marry him. How could I marry a man under my caliber who neither appealed to me nor was I in love with him. A man who hardly brushed his teeth and had problem taking his birth. How can one give a kiss to someone whose teeth was sick and the gums worn out looking green. Although he was tall and fairly good looking but very unkempt, in tattered trousers between the legs. Under normal circumstances, there was no way I would have accepted him for one reason, mainly he was not my type. Moreover, I was deceitfully cajoled to accept his offer on the belief it was God's will as was portrayed by his prayer making me feel I was rejecting my "Mr. Right." Consequently, with a heavy heart, and the intention not to offend God, I dived into the unknown, into the streaming waters with no out-let had God not intervened.

IV. Frying pan into fire

Having got me by evil means to accept his offer, a white wedding took place in a catholic church in 1975. In this union God blessed me with two sons who were my sole comfort during the whole ordeal. They were God's consolation for me. Perhaps, it would be of interest to mention I have always believed, while in secondary school, an elementary school holder who is a devout Christian is more educated than a university graduate who is not a Christian. To be honest, I was not actually interested on the educational background of my prince charming provided he was a Christian. This, to me, was probably the reason the enemy brought me to his agent who was an elementary school holder knowing I would agree to stay with him out of the fear of God. Prior to the wedding, the man ate from my finger, dancing to my tune. Little did I know it was all a camouflage. Not long after, his true color began to manifest, then I realized I have fallen from the frying pan into fire. The threat I should not dare reveal the nature of his prayer to any one I took seriously as I had no intention of going insane. I began to lead a life of a bird in a cage and in terrible fear. How would I face my school friends who had high opinion of my person and great reliance on my good judgement when it comes to the things of the heart. Shame was my constant companion and regret the music in my heart. No-one knew how I felt except the Almighty Father from whose face I fell woefully, without the slightest idea how to reach him except through the man on my side whom I presumed was supposed to be His mouth-piece, so the man portrayed himself to me. I was a sinner, he told me. He was the only one who could pray to obtain me forgiveness as my prayer would not be heard because I bled in the house of God through His priest. I was in a big dilemma, unable to help myself, nobody to confide in. I was in a state of terrible mental stress.

One day to my utter surprise, his prayer instructed he should lie with my daughter Antonia in order to be his biological daughter. This was more than I could bear, yet I could not challenge him as the instruction stared me in the eyes, written in black and white. I wondered if that was his reason to insist and agitate she should come to Germany so as to get used to her brothers while they were still children. It would be good if they all grew up together he insisted. To this end my mother was made to bring her over. I could not help but regret to have succumbed to the idea as I pondered on my heart how God could allow such a thing. He began to lecture me and brain-washed me on why such a thing was very important and essential, supporting himself with the bible and the prayer. Little did I know the incidence quoted from the bible and the steak at hand were not in any way related. However, believing the instruction came directly from God, as usual, there was nothing I could do than to obey. He had such a convincing manner and strong influence over me due to the prayer. It was hell on earth for me and no way out. Little did I know it was all the plan of the evil spirits and their agent Anthony to separate me more from God who hates sin to serve their purpose.

Sometimes it is difficult for someone to understand something not personally experienced, but that does not mean such things do not happen or do not exist. Had I not experienced it I would not have believed it either. Unfortunately, I was so naive to believe everything he told me, but on the other hand who would want to go insane, after seeing such out of the ordinary exhibition, the letters he received from his prayers. Besides, who would want to disobey God if one is raised up with the fear of Go? Nevertheless, as already mentioned, God endowed me with two intelligent boys who with their knowledge, at such tender age, helped to soothe my nerves and eased to some extent the sorrow on my soul. My elder son, Emmanuel, to my utter surprise, defined Albert Einstein's theory of light and expanded it at the age of five. I can still picture him sitting on the kitchen table lecturing me on Einstein. His younger brother, Peter, was not less intelligent. His objective was to become a biologist, as he showed great interest in nature. But these are dreams of yesterday. Being unable to initiate Emmanuel into his secret society won for Emmanuel Anthony's hatred.

Today, I am happy he hated Emmanuel which made him disown him, as son, in his heart. In so doing Anthony lost every right on Emmanuel and caused their separation spiritually. They have no relationship any longer. He became no longer his biological father in the same way Esau lost his birth right to Jacob. This was revealed to me in the dream during a roll call and he was called with my maiden name. As for Peter, Anthony never regarded him as his son from his birth. He systematically disorganized the children, placing them in a state of weak-kneed by addressing them as insane children. "You are insane like your mother" he told them. Occasionally though, to camouflage his meanness, he would include himself as mad, but who has nausea with his own vomit. The children became an outlet to vent his anger over the unattainable wealth he had so much pursued and trusted he would acquire through gambling.

In order to come in possession of wealth there must be peace and harmony in the home, he said. The evil spirits promised him wealth. As usual, of course, I was blamed for being an obstacle to peace and harmony. Having expected to make a "Yes" woman out of me, which was somehow very difficult, as I often had a word or two to say against his escapade, I became for him an insubordinate woman merely because I had an opinion. Besides, he had only to consider my opinion or suggestion and make his decision rather than getting upset and telling me off in very harsh terms. Although he was the one on the way to peace, yet I sought the children's co-operation urging them to tolerate his escapade for a while or at least for three months, having been made to understand "the wealth" was a promise from God. This was an attempt for peace so as to be in wealth and end our long term dependency on social-welfare.

The forfeit of my dreams to settle down with him, uneducated as he was, with impaired hearing, meant nothing to him. His compensation to me was to bully me often into doing whatever I would otherwise not have done. I became a prey to his criticisms, always under the torment of his tongue. I have no flair for fashion he would accuse me, whereas he was supposed to be the provider. I wore what he provided even though they were not my taste. Being a gambler he became a frequent visitor to pawnshops to make ends meet as the family was always lacking in nutriment. Sometimes he would claim the items back, sometimes not. If there was no other opportunity to lay his hands on money to feed the family or to gamble he would go to the social-welfare to create a scene with the officers until he was given some money or food-coupon. On the long run peace was never achieved and there was no wealth, and how could it have been otherwise when he had no fault. Every level-headed being knows it takes two to make a quarrel. It was a very unbearable situation to live with a proud and domineering nagger who could talk for hours on end on any trivial matter. A real personification of selfishness, greed, one who would not hesitate to stoop low, if need be, for his own selfish gains, a pretense for kindness, as he would easily explode at the slightest impression he was being taken for granted. A man with a peculiar character who could not be pleased unless one danced to his tune making life a bore.

The unattainable wealth was for me and my sons a blessing in disguise. A sign of God's Mercy, otherwise, we would have been swimming in the deceit today, held in the bondage of Satan and deprived of our Heavenly Father's Love forever. Anthony's attempt to reach the children diabolically almost exposed his wickedness, on his return to his body, having left it to visit them in their room one night, but God in his infinite mercy shielded them from harm. The children frightened out of their life on the sight of his wicked soul, calling it a strange head, shoved it off, while a bright light covered them like an umbrella. The head then passed through the wall into the adjacent room, the living room where Anthony and I were sleeping on the couch. He detested sleeping in the bedroom. From behind him, where I lay, I was scared out of my life when I woke up to see the ugly thing that looked like a head, with a face resembling that of his father I thought then, hovering in front of him. If I had had the courage to observe it, without screaming, he would have been exposed because I might have seen the apparition enter his body. However, with my screaming the apparition disappeared as he woke up pretending not to have seen anything. This became another source of mental torture and manipulation of the mind for me and my sons to his amusement, we saw a "head" which he did not see, pretending to be innocent of it all. Hardly did I realize his wicked spirit was returning to him having been unsuccessful with whatever he intended to do to my innocent sons, but God's Light shielded them.

Could you imagine a life with someone who had nothing better to talk about than evil spirits, evil eye and people leaving their bodies. I was made to understand there are spirits hovering about that can posses another body if the soul possessing that body delays in returning back to it. A set of encyclopedia, which he ended up not paying for, was purchased for the purpose of educating me on such matters. It was sickening, boring, scaring and of no interest to me. As usual no attention was paid to my resentments. Such stories created great fears in me much to his amusement, as he was bent on having me where he wanted to have me. His intention, I was made to understand, was for us to make Heaven together, but his character and action showed no such intention to me. It was very disheartening hearing his vague explanation, on my persistent accusation he was not acting like a Christian. Once again he silenced me by informing me he knew exactly what I wanted, but would not grant it me until I learnt the lessons he was teaching me. Little did I know he sold his soul to Satan and was cunningly and cleverly working me up to share the same fate with him. Fear was my constant companion and death a scare. I was scared out of my life to accept an apartment in which the former tenant passed away to his amusement. I was his prey and he enjoyed giving me the scare.

His sole hobby was watching horror films, cutting sex pictures and arranging them in albums, filming naked women at the beach, playing machines and gambling. His addiction to sex films turned our store room into his private sex shop. Against my feelings, sex films were for him a normal entertainment to his male visitors during which I would be asked to leave the living room on the pretense he was advertising them for sale. It was to me a source of humiliation which I had to bear that almost tore my heart apart. Watching him leave sex magazines carelessly at the reach of the children, scolding them for watching them or his sex films on video which were left on the floor exposed to their reach, was a great pain which I had to bear, being unable to protect my sons morally. Little did I know he was indirectly modeling them to be addicted to sex as he was, which is Satanic, in order to shake them out of God's Hands. Having made fruitless efforts to put an end to it all I gave up, as each time there was a row, and he could shout and twist things to make one look guilty. Such was my dilemma and I would not wish such a life for any one. It was simply horrible. Not having a way of escape, no means of changing my fate and that of my children I began to live a life of resignation, and submission, out of the fear of God thinking it was God's Will for me if He chose such a person as His servant to be my lot.

In all the tumult there were of course some family get together at his leisure, but very few indeed and always what he himself wanted. Occasionally, there was a visit to the seasonal entertainment park where one is forced to ride scary equipment to his pleasure as he enjoyed the effect they had on one. About two or three times we had a stroll in the woods and about two times to children's playing ground. We drove from city to city, not as entertainment though, but rather for me to go from church to church asking for alms. Our staying permission was threatened then, there was some hopes of obtaining it as the law protects the family, but that was how he chose to spend the time, although he was receiving social help for the maintenance of the family. He bought second hand bicycles for the children and rode out about two or three times with them and that was it. Two or three times we drove out on sight-seeing and ate ice. Once we paddled a canoe on the Alster and once with Emmanuel when I was in the hospital at the birth of Peter, my younger son. There were some family video films and photographs taken. All these were at the time when the children were under ten as he still entertained the hope of initiating Emmanuel into his secret society. It was his wish for Emmanuel to possess the gift of prayer and hand it over to his future son, a type of inheritance for the next generation.

Having been deceived it was of God I blindly had no objection to it. Who would not want to be that close to God. But to his disappointment, Emmanuel's spirit did not accept his plan and he turned against him. For this reason Emmanuel became more or less his enemy and was never able to please him. To justify his animosity towards him, Anthony took advantage of the poor child's misconduct at school, when, in his second year at primary school, in his folly, he cut, with a scissors, a bit of hair from a girl in his class. He finished the poor child up with his sharp tongue making him feel so wretched and unloved. The child could not understand the much ado over what for him was a mere joke. How his heart broke and mine ached for him. I was helpless. His entire childhood became a nightmare and his unhappiness almost broke my heart. How could one who calls himself a father shout, with such animosity, at his child, a minor, still under ten years old, as though they were mates. Anthony never failed to seize every opportunity to pick up quarrel with Emmanuel and always made a drop of water a mighty ocean. This sorry situation went on into the teenage age of my poor sons which caused me great fears they might ultimately become insane as he continuously alluded had the Almighty God not kept a loving watchful gaze on us despite my wretchedness.

Sometimes, when ego tends to dominate the sense of reasoning, pride taking control over humanity, then one dares permit himself, in the ugliness of its luxury, to assume one owns the world, as nothing else matters but self, then does Providence extend a helping hand, allowing suffering, pull one down to earth. Him whom the father loves he chastises therefore, God in His infinite Mercy, being madly in love with us provides us, His beloved children, always a way of escape from the evil enticement of Satan. As God's being is Love He does not change our free-will. The choice is entirely ours to reciprocate His love and console the Heavenly Father who infinitely loves us. It is very unfortunate though, some have sold their souls to Satan turning deaf ears to the Father's warning, making Satan their choice on their own free-will. The main objective of the soul is love, being part of God who is love therefore, the soul hungers for love. In the quest for love humanity is confronted with counterfeit of it polished in glittery camouflage, by Satan, for the enticement of souls whose dependency rests on materialism. Such souls reject the pure Holy, True, Faithful and Eternal Love of God. Souls who desire the pomp and riches of this world reject Eternal Life with God to choose Satan who is evil and eternal death. To such unfortunate souls Anthony belonged. He had ample opportunities to step out of Satan's trap, but he would not dare for reasons best known to him. He knew the bible well enough but for his own purpose. How fatal it is to put a deaf ear to God's call, the sweet loving Father of humanity, for the riches and pomp of this transitory world. There would be no turning back when death knocks at the door but to face God's justice.

On July 1995 we moved into a bigger apartment as the children got into their teenage age to enable them have a room to themselves respectively. Little did I know the Hand of Providence was leading and guiding me to the choice of the apartment I made. It was the Holy Will of God the apartment should be registered under my name. As events would have it, after the apartment was found Anthony was supposed to sign the tenants' contract, but in his usual way of showing who the boss was, he drove me there and preferred to wait for me in the car while I went in to the Estate Agency and signed the contract. Hardly did I realize the role this was to play later in my life. My main concern was to move out of the apartment that brought me and the children so much misery with the hope of experiencing some happiness as a married woman and mother by watching my children attain whatever joy left for them in their parental home to sustain them in their adulthood when they would begin to taste the hardships of life on their own feet.

Unfortunately this hope was shattered, we began to dance to the same old tune of Anthony's tyranny, mishandling of the children, in the pretense of being a good father. He had the right training method he said. That the neighbors could hear his voice, very loud, filled with animosity, as though he was having a row with strangers, did not bother him. My efforts to draw his attention to it, to the sound of his voice remained, each time, fruitless as he had no respect for any one. No one is good but himself. He made himself notorious, both at the court and at the social-welfare, the source of his livelihood, he was able to play his cards well from being detected of his laziness to work. When his aggressiveness and animosity became unbearable for the children to cope with, having threatened them with a knife, the last straw that broke the camel's back, scared out of their life they arranged with the social-welfare and left home, without notice, shortly before Christmas of 1995. You can just imagine the state of my mind as a mother. The whereabouts of my children whose presence was a consolation to me, was kept secret. It was with a heavy heart the children left as their main concern was my well-being. They had hoped Anthony would come to his right mind and realize he was not a good father and at least be kind to me. They were wrong. He did not care, rather threatened and forbade me from picking up the receiver if the children telephoned. However, after Christmas Emmanuel telephoned to ask if he could come home to talk with Anthony, reluctantly he accepted. But to my utter surprise and dismay, his coming met with such indifference, lack of understanding for his motive to have left home with his brother. All Anthony cared about was his image. It was a disgrace to him that his children, children he had no regard for, left home. Emmanuel, who came with the hope for the room to apologize, left with

Bless the Lord, all his works, in all places of his dominion. Bless the Lord O my soul!"

On reading this psalm I felt God was speaking directly to me and I felt a certain peace and joy in my heart and immediately I felt Anthony would not die. Consequently, I informed his younger brother, Andrew, also living in Hamburg and my children, telling them he would not die. On the long run, God saved his life and spared my mother. Hardly did I know my mother was very sick at the time and on the point of death, but God in his infinite mercy saved her life. My father informed me on phone, when I called to inform him about Anthony's ailment, my mother was also sick, but she miraculously recovered. This was more than a clear sign of God's mercy. I simply said to my father "I know." My mother would probably have died, but due to my innocent prayer, our Heavenly Father, God of Mercy saved her life.

This was the beginning of my realization God can hear my prayer, then I began gradually to wake out of slumber. Anthony could no longer stop me from attending mass due to his disability, although the attempt was made. In the course of time, without knowing how, my life was transformed and I realized I have developed a personal relationship with God the Father, God the Son, to the Blessed Virgin Mary, my Mum. The Holy Spirit lit the Flame of Love burning deep in my Heart for my God.

The awareness of God's love began gradually to dawn on me. I began receiving the sacrament of reconciliation, without confessing the former sins which were confessed to Anthony. The sins committed in the union with him were not confessed due to the fact I did not regard them as sins as I still thought he had access to God through his gift of prayer. Our parish priest came once a month to bring him communion. When I think of it now I cannot help but wonder how he could dare receive communion without the sacrament of reconciliation, bearing on mind what Jesus said about those who would receive Him unworthily. Anyway, according to him, he would be standing at the gate of Heaven ushering people in. He had answer to everything and cannot make mistakes he made clear to me and my sons.

I must not fail to mention the part Andrew, Anthony's younger brother, played. I have always had great regard for him taking him to be educated, more enlightened than his brother and decent. I felt pity for him for his inability of securing himself a wife after his first wife, an English woman, left him leaving him with a son, Chukwuma, about two years old. I assisted him with the upbringing of Chukwuma. This was a help to enable him do his work as a cab driver, the job he picked up, being unable to cope with his profession as a chemist so he would bring the child over to me. However, he did not do badly as a cab driver, having been able, in the course of time, to purchase a cab and drive for himself. In his desperation for a soul-mate he thought he found one in Catherine, a girl-friend of mine. But this relationship was not fated to function and Catherine deserted him before they could marry leaving him with a baby girl, Jean, under one year old. Once more I had to offer my help. At this time his son Chukwuma was about four years old and attending a nursery school. Jean was living with me and I nursed her as though she was my biological child.

About two and a half years later, Andrew happened to discover, and got to know of a cousin of mine Chizua. He became interested in her and expressed the desire to marry her. My humility and subordination to his brother impressed him, so he hoped someone from my family, considering our Christian Faith, would be ideal for him for a wife. Therefore, he instigated me, with his persistence, to inform my mother who consequently informed Chizua's mother. A widow, who consented, on the belief my in-laws must have a high opinion of me to want to marry a relation of mine.Moreover, she felt it would be better if her daughter married into a family where she would not be a total stranger because of me, so Chizua's photograph was sent to Andrew and he sent his to her. On seeing Chizua's photograph, a pretty girl of about twenty-eight years old, tall, athletic, fair in complexion with a taste for fashion, Andrew was swept off his feet with admiration. He could not wait for her arrival, so with alacrity arrangements were completed to that effect. What would have taken about six months to complete was rushed through within a month.

Travelling to and fro, from Enugu to Cotonou, and from Enugu to Benin to enable Andrew's elder brother, who had his residence there, to know her before she joined him in Germany and back to Enugu, was very hectic and tiresome. This was a result of the hardships connected with public transportation, due to bad conditions of roads, including the burning heat of the sun, which left their signature on Chizua causing her to lose weight. Andrew who was bursting with excitemeant and expectation, got himself drunk with disappointment, disinterest and lack of understanding, when Chizua finally arrived in the spring of 1999. He did not find her as attractive as she was in her picture, he grumbled. His failure to realize she needed to freshen up after a long flight, his lack of sympathy for her loss of weight, which was his fault, he made her run helter-skelter, from city to city, country to country on his errand, in a short duration, eager for her arrival, made me realize his small mind. All he could do was to complain bitterly she arrived in sport shoes, canvas shoes as he called them. Without hesitation, making no accommodation for her to settle down and regain her weight, Andrew arranged for her return back to Nigeria. Thoughtless of the humiliation it will cause her on her return to Nigeria, having called off her engagement to marry someone there for Andrew because of me. It was sad and heart-breaking for Chizua. To my utter surprise and dismay, Andrew expected me to show sympathy for him. How I suffered in silence. However, Chizua somehow assessed the whole situation, realizing my handicap that was my consolation.

However, instead of travelling back to Nigeria Chizua, in her utter confusion, informed a cousin, an American military officer based in

Aschaffenburg – Germany, about her situation, who invited her to Aschaffenburg with the intention of sending her to the United States, to a relation who is an American citizen to save her the embarrassment of returning to Nigeria. While waiting for the completion of the arrangements for her travel to the United States, Chizua needed an extension of her German visa. For this purpose my assistance was sought to escort her to the immigration. As Anthony had no German residence permit he opened a shipping and forwarding Agency with Andrew's name, his younger brother, who has German citizenship, due to his marriage with Chukwuma's mother who was English. The registration of the firm as a family enterprise was a camouflage. It was entirely his firm. I was made to work there as the secretary. That notwithstanding, Chizua called the office line in my absence to inform me of her intention to extend her German visa and to ask for my assistance. Unfortunately, as events would have it Anthony received the call in my absence.

Rather than informing me about the purpose of Chizua's call first, Anthony chose to inform his brother whose fiery temper was an open book. Just as was expected, Andrew threatened to stop Chizua from extending her visa. How could he dare, I thought, having rejected her and sent her away from his home. After all, the least he could do for her, was to allow her patch up the broken pieces of her life, having turned down an engagement while relying on his promises to marry her. But no, Andrew would not let her be until she paid him every penny he spent on her to bring her to Germany. In his opinion she should have sought his permission before seeking for an extension of visa. Would he have granted it her? How could I ever have thought him to be a gentleman. Perhaps, the dog life I led with his brother gave me no room to realize there could be no difference between apples of the same tree. Had things been otherwise I may have saved Chizua all the trouble. Unfortunately nobody can influence fate except God if His help is sought.

To my utter surprise, on our arrival at the immigration, there was Andrew, charged like an angry lion. With such fury he tried to prevent Chizua from entering into the waiting-room. His aggression drew the attention of everyone as he shouted antagonistically, regardless of the crowded room. Had I not witnessed it myself, I would never have believed he could exhibit such fury in public. What a disgrace he caused himself with such display of temper against a harmless innocent girl he hurt without remorse. That all eyes were on him charging against a harmless girl did not bother him. All he cared for was his demand for twenty-five thousand Naira, about two hundred Deutsche Mark, today about hundred Euro. Had it not been for the crowd he would have attacked her physically. This incidence changed my opinion about him as I realized education alone does not make a gentleman. However, the crowd was able to direct his attention away from Chizua. Nevertheless, Chizua was able to procure an extended visa, grateful the situation did not extend to physical attack, but it was a shocking experience for her as she was not used to such an outburst of temper.

Having failed to achieve his aim to stop Chizua from extending his visa Andrew came furiously to the office, not caring the customers in the office he snatched his daughter Jean, then two and half years old, from my arms. However, he first exchanged angry words with his elder brother Anthony who sprayed gas on his face to stop any physically attack. The two brothers were cat and mouse, very quick tempered. All I had for Andrew was pity. Nobody would like to be in the shoes of someone unable to show gratitude to the woman who helped him raise his two children, no matter what she must have done to him, after all one's good turn deserves another. His inability to forgive me for escorting Chizua to the immigration made him hostile to his brother so he jeopardized the shipping and forwarding agency registered under his name. Transient is the smile of fate, so it was for Anthony's firm which had no future. His lack of knowledge on shipping and forwarding, being a gambler, already spelt failure for the firm. Besides, his gambling activities did not escape the observation of his customers as he made no secret about it. The people he called customers were actually not customers. Who would want to trust his goods to a gambler. No, they did their shipment, several cars and containers, with some reliable agents, but maintained their relationship with him for the technical help and free lunch they received from him. As camouflage, they would bring him a car for shipment. But few people who were unaware of his gambling brought him goods only to desert him immediately as soon as they became aware he was a gambler. Anthony, on his part, thought he was advertising, with the free lunch, the firm that was destined for bankruptcy.

The public exhibition of Andrew's anger disclosed to me the reason for his incapability of finding a soul-mate. All the women in his life left him. After the incident with Chizua he dated a girl from his home town in Nigeria, married and brought her to Germany. A beautiful girl of about twenty-eight years old, plump, average in height and fair in complexion. He appeared to be in competition with his elder brother aiming at procuring a wife of my caliber who would be submissive to him as I was to his brother. Little did he realize I was born and bred by parents who loved God, held in captive by his wicked brother, an agent of evil spirits. If Andrew was aware of his brother's practices I would not know. All I knew was his worry about the early death of his family members, one after the other, and his belief something was buried in their compound causing their early death. To this effect he sought in vain for a pastor who would pray in his father's compound for the removal of whatever was buried there. Anthony bragged his people were dying due to his absence in Nigeria and that people around him would not easily die. In other words his presence prevents those around him from dying. In his own words "Andrew is still alive because he is in Hamburg where I am because his death will pain me". He believed he would not die early, he would live up to hundred years. This made me feel happy then, believing I would at least not die early, without realizing the danger I was in and with whom I was dealing.

Well, Andrew's new wife, Chizie, deserted him, after giving him three beautiful daughters. However, she left him with her children to London. She could not cope with his anger and physical attacks any longer. His attempts to bring her against me failed. Having painted me black before her made her drop the telephone on me while talking with her about the condition of Anthony, during his time in the rehabilitation center.

However, before talking with Chizie I spoke first with Andrew but he dropped the phone on me. Thereafter, I called a second time and got his wife on the line. In the attempt to protect the integrity of Anthony whose urine catheter was removed to check if he could urinate independently without the catheter, I asked them to visit him the following day after the urine catheter has been replaced, seeing the way he was going about with his private part which was not decent to the eyes. Nevertheless, the suggestion Andrew could visit him alone if he wanted, being a man and his brother won me Andrew's animosity. However, it was not surprising to me he told me off and dropped the phone on me as it was his habit whenever he felt like it. As I feared being left alone with Anthony in his ailment, I decided to explain to them the reason I made that suggestion in the attempt to make them understand me. Therefore, I called back later, his wife picked the phone, but Andrew asked her to drop it. I could hear him command her to do so. On my next attempt Jean picked the phone, but had to drop it on command. It hurt me because I regarded her as my daughter.

That not withstanding, somehow I was able to phone in his absence and his wife picked the phone without hanging up on me. It was then she disclosed to me Andrew's ill opinion about me to which I responded, "If I am what he said I am then I would not have been able to assist him in raising up his son and his daughter". It was then she exclaimed with surprise informing me she was not told. Patiently I explained to her the reason I did not want her to visit Anthony that day to which she gave me her understanding so we let sleeping dogs lie and became friends. We both condemned the scene Andrew made at the rehabilitation center the following Sunday when he visited Anthony with his family. As usual, after feeding Anthony with his lunch I helped him to his wheelchair and drove him to the sink to tidy him up. At this moment Andrew walked into the room, without ceremony he suddenly snatched his brother from me without my permission, ignoring the attention I was giving to him. In my surprise, at the manner he carried himself, I said he should have waited until I finished with his brother before taking him only to realize my utterance spelt trouble. He shouted in such a fury insulting me for nothing. The nurses gathered around calming him down, informed him it was a rehabilitation center and noise was prohibited. What a nightmare! I could not understand what I did to deserve such insolence and disrespect. Somehow the nurses managed to make him take his leave. From then on he seized visiting his brother, left me alone to cope with it all. I found it strange wondering at the kind of brotherly love they share.

Knowing fully well Andrew would not come to see his brother the day he was discharged I phoned him earlier to apologize for what happened even though I saw no fault of mine, but for the sake of peace besides, I felt Anthony would be pleased. In fact apologizing was a daily habit of mine in that family as both Andrew and Anthony led me a dog's life. The only alternative I had for a little peace was to apologize for everything, but inwardly prayed for God's mercy for it was indeed a dog's life I led. Andrew's wife later took me into confidence informing me of the bad state of her marriage and her intention to desert her husband. That did not surprise me knowing Andrew as I did, but being still in the dark about Anthony's relationship with evil spirits I gave her a Christian advice to endure for Christ as I was doing.

She was aware of Anthony's cruelty to me and made it clear to me she would not tolerate disrespect and cruelty. My refusal to support her to desert her husband made her carry out her intention without informing me. Nevertheless, she got in touch with me from her London residence after my separation from Anthony. We both expressed our gratitude to God for being able to lose ties from that family we both believe is cursed. She would have liked to change her name to her maiden name but for the complications therefore, for the moment she decided to wait for a better opportunity. As for me I had no hesitation to taking back my maiden name to which she expressed her surprise I was able to get it done. I informed her it was all God's mercy and she was happy for me.

To start life afresh, I had to apologize to everyone I must have offended, unintentionally, during the horrible life with Anthony. I made a phone call to the court and apologized to the lady judge for the nasty letters I was compelled to write for Anthony to her and to her colleagues. To my relief I was informed they were all aware of my condition. My apology was rendered also to all the social well-fare officials directly connected to the insolence made to them at Anthony's command and for the badly worded letters, so this way I was able to clear myself for a life with Jesus.

VI. The Separation

It is commonly known Satan can never be pleased and the same thing applies to his agents who have sold their souls to him. However one tried to please there must be complaint one way or the other. Such people who serve Satan take one for granted and are never grateful. Should one be wrong once, dealing with them, the ten times when one was not wrong are forgotten and one must pay through one's nose for that very wrong. So is Satan and their agents. They do not believe in Goodness and Mercy. All they know is pretense, flamboyance, for they are green snakes in green grass. They pretend to be angels of light while they are instruments of darkness. Evil does exist and should be exposed. If one did not experience evil one tends to doubt its existence, but the fact God himself revealed to man the existence of evil, paid a heavy price to liberate man from evil is a great evidence to believe in the existence of evil. To deny the existence of evil is to make God a liar and anyone who denies the existence of evil has not the Truth in himself.

As I began to attend the Holy Mass, receive the Sacraments of Reconciliation and the Holy Eucharist my life began to experience the effects of the Sacraments. That Anthony is evil began gradually to dawn on me for his character could not possibly be of God. The boldness to challenge his authority and influence over me became evident. Although, my resentment of him was not fully at its best, as I still felt he was my cross and bore patiently his wickedness, he was no longer able to compel me to implement everything he said at will. My reasoning began to be effective. However, I did not realize then my challenge of his attitude was due to my weekly attendance of the mass and the reception of the Sacraments. Nevertheless, the more I challenged him the more ugly he became in the attempt to suppress me.

In the year 2001 I began taking my own initiative. Against his will I insisted on visiting my aged parents for the first time after twenty-eight years. Before now, I was not allowed to do so. He would not visit home himself either, with a lame excuse he was afraid to fly. Ignorantly I bought that from him, although there was nothing I could have done otherwise, but in retrospect I believe it was merely an excuse to keep me from bothering him about visiting home. The few attempts to raise the issue always ended up in a big row. How could he afford the money, he would argue citing his dependent on the social-welfare, forgetting the family allowance he threw into gambling. Had he actually made it his objective to visit home, from the family allowance, if properly managed, he could have afforded to make small savings, which would eventually have been, in the course of time, enough to finance the flight.

However, it happened that during the golden jubilee celebration of my parents in 2000 my parents expected me to come home, but Anthony's condition, was an impediment to my travel. The actual year of the golden jubilee of my parents was 1997 but postponed to 2000, probably for the convenience of my brothers living in the United States to enable them attend. Nevertheless, being unable to attend I sent Peter, my younger son who was then twenty-two years old to represent me. On his return, I realized, after watching the video films he brought, my parents had grown old and I developed a certain urge to visit them. Just as was expected, Anthony tried, to no avail, to coarse me, with his domineering tactics, into not travelling. I loved my parents very much, seeing them age under my very nose, the inability to do anything for them, as their eldest daughter, after the love and affection they gave me while I was growing up, became a burden which I carried in my heart in silence.

Having made up my mind to visit my parents I was determined not to allow him play on me as he did in spring of 1991 when he sent me to Lagos, thinking his bread was buttered he would become a millionaire, to meet some swindler who thought he had a flourishing firm and hoped to make him their prey. After a formidable lecture, how to behave in Lagos with his so called business partners, he forbade me to visit my parents in Enugu. He managed to convince me we were all to travel together in summer of the same year therefore, it was better for the whole family to visit home together after being away for so long. As I was living then in great fear, I believed the key to my safe flight to and fro was only obedience to him bearing on mind, as he made me believe, God was with him and I was a sinner whose sins were not yet forgiven. Emmanuel, my elder son, who was then fourteen years old escorted me.

The subjection to the fear of his threats, should I act contrary to his instructions, prevented me from visiting my parents. Not even the knowledge of my mother's illness could move me to visit them, due to the fear I had of Anthony and his prayer. Matthew Jr. my parents youngest child, who was six years old when I left home to go through many waters, now twenty-six, staying with the relations we put up with in Lagos, Mr. and Mrs. Anya, expressed surprise I turned down the invitation to visit our sick mother. Little did he know what I had to put up with which I could not relate to any one for fear of going insane as I was made to believe. The poor boy thought it was love when I refused to dance at the night club he took me and Emmanuel to, believing I was missing Anthony. He never knew how my heart ached for not being able to visit my sick mother. How I missed my parents!

However, this time events were different. He was on a wheelchair, still a tyrant, abusive as usual and aggressive. A relation of mine, Fidelis, watching the treatment he give me, in his presence, developed high blood pressure after his constant visit, due to his inability to help me out. His observation of the lack of respect and humiliation I received in silence was too much for him to bear. Before now Fidelis assumed my world was at peace and knowing Anthony's suspicious mind he kept his distance, as he did not want to involve himself in family problem, but on hearing of Anthony's stroke he decided to pay him a visit. On seeing I needed some support he made himself a frequent visitor and came to realize I was in supe. All his attempts to make me see Anthony's wickedness was to no avail. I did not blame him as I always defended Anthony, not because I did not realize the absurdity in his character, I did not want to wash any dirty linen in public, besides, I wanted to carry my cross.

Having failed to make me see reason, Fidelis stopped visiting but kept contact with me on phone much to Anthony's displeasure. After several unfruitful attempts to stop me from receiving calls from Fidelis, he began ironically, to portray Fidelis as evil, insisting I was ignorant of his true color hoping this way to convince me to distance myself from him. During this time Fidelis was struggling with his residence permit therefore, Anthony assumed he would be deported due to his wickedness. However, as God would have it nothing of the sought happened which made me began paying less attention to his discredit of people. Had Fidelis evil inclinations he would have been deported, but as his hands were clean, he had no illegal records, our good God had mercy, leaving for me the only close relation I have here in Germany. Nevertheless, I realized later the reason Anthony was uncomfortable with my association with Fidelis was his fears Fidelis might make me see through his cloak and realize his own wickedness. Fidelis found it unbearable watching me suffer for nothing. The man who could not respect his sister in his presence, blind and ungrateful to her efforts did not deserve his respect which he would not have hesitated to make clear to him had it not been his respect for my feelings. Therefore, for his own health he ceased to visit.

That not withstanding, Anthony could not stop me from travelling to Nigeria to visit my aging parents. I flew home to my parents in 2001 with Emmanuel which was a blessing in disguise for little did I know it was the last time I was to see my father who departed to his Savior in December 2006 at the age of ninety-one, after fifty-nine years of marriage to my mother. If I did not pay heed to the threats of Anthony, the servant of the evil spirits under the camouflage of a servant of God with his great knowledge of the Bible, I would have met my father again before his departure. My father desired my return during Christmas of 2006. Four days after Christmas he went Home to God, his Father. In my eagerness to see him again, I promised him I would, but Anthony's ugly nagging and criticisms hindered the motivation to struggle for a travelling document. Unfortunately, due to his constant insulting letters to the court, our resident permit was withdrawn when several warnings could not induce him to stop writing.

However, it hurt me badly to disappoint my father whose voice could not hide from me, how disappointed he felt, when I informed him it would not be possible for me, after all, to make it. We had planned, on my return, I should take him to the Catholic Church. He accepted to be in the same Church with me, to be Catholic. To this end I was to come home. Nevertheless, somehow, I felt he understood my predicament, the reason for my inability to come home. When he blessed all his children on the occasion of the opening of the family house in the village, he asked God to grant me happiness for I have suffered enough. During this occasion my brothers living in the United States and my sisters were there except me. Lawrence, the elder son, returned with his family. From the recorded tape of this event, sent to me by my immediate younger sister Ifeoma, I could hear my Father's blessing. When my father began to call me "My Hope" each time we were on phone little did I realize he was preparing me for his departure. That my parents would one day depart from this world was a fairy-tale. I never gave thought to it so, my father's departure took me by surprise for I loved him very much.

Anthony, a dog in a manger, who lead someone a dog's life, took his disablement for granted with the aim to ruin my life. That he began writing insulting letters to social-welfare office demanding equipment he was not ready to use was his strategy to ruin my life, feeling no harm would come to him due to his disablement. After all, I was the unfortunate instrument used for such ugly letters who should be held responsible as he was disabled, but Providence was on my side. To every rejected application he made to the social well-fare he followed with appeals to the court, written in the nastiest language one could think of, which eventually instigated the judges, especially the lady judge who had the worst of it, to see to the withdrawal of our permanent visa. Although an appeal was made, it was an uncomfortable situation to the delight of Anthony, who bullied me and prophesied my deportation. He bragged saying "no one would bother a disabled person like me" It was then I realized his tricks and his wickedness, but then it was too late. There was no way I could put back the clock, the deed was done.

However, If I had the slightest idea of his evil intentions, I would perhaps, not have bothered his nagging, the trouble he would have made the whole day and refused to write those letters. He had the undaunted notion the insulting words in his letters were the language best suited to bring the court succumb to his demands, due to the psychological effect it was meant to have on the judges. How could telling everyone off, using God's name in vain, evidence of the animosity in his heart, his unforgiving spirit towards his offenders, be diplomacy. It was most unfortunate I could not realize his sick mind and his wickedness earlier. My only consolation is God's Mercy, reaching out to me and embracing me, while still in this vale of tears, to prepare me for eternity with Jesus in Heaven where I will be forever happy in His loving Arms without any more sorrows. As for Anthony, according to him, he would report his offenders to God and prevent them from entering into heaven. He would never forgive them even in death. How could such a one be a Christian. The fear of his words instigated me and my children write his ugly letters in order to have room to breathe. Oh, how my heart ached for my innocent sons for such a father who was not a father.

This was the prevailing situation that influenced my inability to travel home at my father's request being without traveling documents. However, after my father's departure, on the twenty-ninth of December 2006, it became urgent and inevitable for me to obtain a travelling document for my father's burial ceremony. I needed a substitute passport from the immigration for this purpose. Prior to the withdrawal of our residence permit I was already in the procedure for German citizenship therefore, my Nigerian passport was withheld at the Nigerian embassy for renouncing my Nigerian citizenship. After several attempts to procure the substitute passport proved to no avail I was frustrated and depressed for being denied the opportunity to give my father the last honor being his eldest child.

To my utter surprise and delight my father appeared to me in the dream looking very young in his early thirties, wearing a pink pajamas. He opened the bonnet of a car giving me the impression he was repairing something there. He then asked me to get ready to celebrate his retirement. On waking up I pondered in my heart what the dream could mean, at the same time pleased at the serenity of his presence and knew he is in Heaven. However, when I got to the immigration that day, to my utter surprise, the substitute passport stamped with visa was handed over to me without any further harassment. There was no longer the demand to sign a document, as proof to the court, I had given up the pursuit of the appeal against the withdrawal of my residence permit. That was their demand, to trap me, I thought, therefore, I was reluctant to comply with it. My two younger brothers, Lawrence and Matthew Jr., living in the United States, informed me my father also appeared to them in the dream respectively, prior to his departure, to inform them he was ready to retire, also in a pink pajamas and looking very young. This instigated Matthew Jr. who was disposed at the time, to travel home making it possible for him to be present at my father's departure.

I was made to understand my father was very happy at the presence of Matthew Jr. his youngest child to whom he gave his name, Matthew. He was always smiling at the presence of his youngest child. His departure was a peaceful one. As usual, he carried out his daily routine, in the sequence he did them every morning, his morning prayers, his toiletries, his breakfast, read his Bible, eased himself, and asked for his walking stick which was brought to him as he then sank into the arms of my mother and my immediate younger sister Ifeoma who were beside him. He was then carried into the car and rushed to the hospital by Matthew Jr. Little did they know he was already gone to His Jesus as they were all taken by surprise, on their arrival at the hospital, only to be informed by the doctor their father was gone. It was a peaceful departure into the Glory of his Beloved Savior Jesus Christ in eternal joy.

Having recovered from the shock of my father's departure which reduced me to tears for several months on the thought of him, being quite unprepared when it happened, a certain assurance and joy he is in Heaven filled my heart. Anthony's wicked tongue could not rob me of it. How well do I remember the day the information of his departure reached me. Being unaware of what was to be, I went out cheerfully, the day before, to buy a telephone card to call him, telling an acquaintance of mine I met at the bus stop, Jenne from Cameroun, joyfully, I was on my way to buy a phone card to call my parents. So you can simply understand why my ears could not believe what they heard when Ifeoma and Matthew Jr. called to give me the sad news. Although, they tried to put it to me as nice as possible, assuring me he had no pain, as he had no ailment, but I could not help my tears. I was to understand, at my inquiry to know if my father remembered me on the day of his departure and was reminded he did, for he always addressed my mother lovingly as "Mama Hope". That was a consolation more or less.

However, the sad news called to mind the dream I had earlier on in which every member of the family, all relations, distant and near, friends and well-wishers came home to the village for a big celebration. The whole place was filled up with a sea of people, everyone happily enjoying the celebration. I did not realize then it was the burial ceremony of my father I dreamt of. Nevertheless, I know the Almighty Father could not have given me a better father to raise me up for Him in this exile. I will always be grateful to God for his choice of a father for me and for receiving him into His Eternal Glory. He was Heaven's blessing for me in this exile having embedded in me the Christian belief. His love for his wife Flora, for us his children and his humility was a mirror of God's fatherly love and Humility. In him, I believe, the family has an intercessor in Heaven, as he is one of the uncanonized saints of our Beloved Savior Jesus Christ.

Anthony was at his best when he created fear in those under him or caused others to be afraid. It was his pleasure to treat the family as his regiment, himself the general. No one dared oppose him for fear he would blow his top. The consequence of being subjected to the terror of his tongue was no one's cup of tea. Besides, the nagging which could last the whole day was a dread. His disability did not bring any change in him for the better rather his wickedness became more pronounced. His intention was to remain disabled as he began enjoying the care that was given to him. Although he could go independently to toilette, he insisted on being helped, at the same time giving instructions how he was to be kept clean, whereas he could do that himself with his left hand which was not affected.

That not withstanding, he would, sometimes, not want to sit on the wheelchair to be taken to the toilet, but rather preferred to simply do his business in the pampers which he insisted on wearing, while lying down on the couch. Whenever he felt like grumbling about anything or to find out my whereabouts in the apartment, if I was not in his presence to be ushered about, he would get up, sit himself on his wheelchair to satisfy his curiosity. But to go to the bathroom for his birth or for his business, he would not dare. Instead he preferred taking his birth on the couch, causing me much discomfort, despite the bathing-lift at his disposal, for which he insulted both the social-welfare and the court to obtain. In his opinion I was being paid to take care of him so I should work for what I was paid for. A lame excuse for his wickedness. He was quite aware I was not actually paid for it, but compensated with a small allowance for taking care of a family member. Besides, the allowance was also to his favor, as it was also used for his maintenance, for his feeding. Although I knew a trained health care help would be paid a full salary, which would have been a relief for me, I knew none of them would have tolerated him as I did. That not withstanding, I was also subjected, under his terrible tongue, which was sharper than razor, to tolerate him, bearing on mind my Christian principles. It was amazing I did not break down. Had it not been for the Mercy of God, anyone who knew me would not have recognized me anymore. The load I carried was indeed too much for me. My strength was drawn in the belief it was my cross.

All his attempts to make me deviate from my belief my father is alive in Christ's Glory was to no avail. That touched his nerve. I have always believed, Jesus Himself said it, God is not the God of the dead but of the living therefore, knowing the humble life my father lived, in the fear of God, always conscious of His precepts, he could not possibly be any other place than by his Savior whom he loved very dearly. Surprisingly Anthony never bothered about his departed relations, if they were in Heaven or in hell. When several attempts to bring him to pray for his deceased relations was to no avail I refrained from asking him. The much I could do was to say the Divine Mercy prayer for them. Once his only sister, deceased, appeared to me in the dream, nude. On returning home with a girl-friend I saw her in the bathroom, wretched like someone who needed help. I never had the opportunity to know her in this life, only through her picture, so I decided to offer the only help I could, the Divine Mercy prayer and I believe it helped her.

Anthony made a fruitless attempt to ruin the good relationship that existed between me and his elder brother, Ben, who usually took sides with me and cautioned him to give me a better treatment. That was the brother who would not receive me in Lagos, but did so after I persisted. On his last visit to Hamburg in January 2001 Anthony gave him the impression I was stubborn and insubordinate. Although, during his visit he supported my idea to visit my parents in Nigeria, seeing they have grown old, but when he got to Nigeria he sent a fax asking Anthony to travel with me, due to a preacher he found who could make him walk again. The fax, was intended as a means to prevent me from travelling, I thought. Well, I realized there was no means for extra ticket, coupled with the inconvenience of travelling with Anthony who was such a bore therefore, I was disinterested for any further arrangements that would include him. Nevertheless, having realized it was God's Holy Will that I travel I could not tolerate any obstacle.

That not withstanding, initially reservation was made for everyone, including Anthony, though I did not know how to cope with him and how the trip was to be financed. As God would have it Anthony declined, and I was left with Emmanuel with whom I travelled. Peter was not considered, although reservation was also made for him. I felt my bread buttered when Anthony declined. Peter having been to Nigeria for the Jubilee of my parents also declined to reduce the expenditure. In order to avoid unpleasant interrogation in Lagos by Anthony's elder brother Ben, as to why he did not return with me, I wrote to inform him there was no way I could come with him due to financial difficulties, informing him also of his disinterest in travelling. I tried to make him understand every arrangement for his comfort was already completed in a rehabilitation center during my one month absence. Besides, if he persisted on his brother returning with me he should provide the means for his flight and make an alternative arrangements for him should Anthony on the long run still decline to travel, because my mind was set on travelling. Unfortunately, my letter and its aim was misunderstood. For this reason he failed to come to welcome me at the airport, but his two grown up daughters did and informed me he was out of town.

Well, I swallowed it up but his daughters, observing my disappointment, informed me of their father's displeasure over my letter. However, the excitement of seeing my parents, visiting my father's house after twenty-eight years with my son, left no room for any other consideration, so after expressing my gratitude for their coming to welcome me and my son at the airport, my youngest sister, Evelyn, resident at the time with her husband and children in Lagos, in whose house we stayed, drove us home to their end. On the following day we travelled with the bus to Enugu.

It was a happy reunion with my loving parents who, though now advanced in age, could not hide their delight for the arrival of their eldest daughter, the child they dote on and would not cease from praying for her well-being. My mother prayed to be alive when I returned home, so one could imagine how happy she was on seeing me again in the four walls of my parental home accompanied by my elder son Emmanuel, her grandson, who due to his good disposition won at once the heart of his grandparents. After a wonderful time in Enugu, the town of my birth, with my parents, sisters and relatives, we travelled back to my sister Evelyn in Lagos where we spent few days before flying back to Germany. As God would have it, on arrival in Lagos, before flying back to Germany, I insisted on seeing Anthony's elder brother, Ben, even if he was not ready to see me. His daughters who came to see me at my sister's end drove Emmanuel and me to see their father who was not at home when we came, but we waited in his neighbors' apartment until he came back. In the course of the conversation I got to know the source of his anger. Why he believed Anthony, I would not know, probably due to his disability. Well, it was then I gathered Anthony told him, during his visit, I was stubborn and insubordinate. He made me understand he did not believe it then as I did not abandon him to his fate in a home for the disabled, but the contents of my letter was the last straw that broke the camel's back.

To have some witnesses to the contents of the letter a copy of it was sent to his wife who was then in the U.S. staying with one of his daughters, who assured me there was nothing wrong with the letter. Fidelis, my brother, also saw nothing wrong with it. Realizing he did not really know his brother, my unfortunate position of not being able to explain to him, due to his brother's threat with my insanity, if I exposed his secret, made me take every blame but not without telling him he was wrong about me. However, before we took our leave, I embraced him asking him to forget it all and grant me his forgiveness. One of his daughters, the eldest, Bibian, informed me that gesture was like a tonic on her father's nerves. Thereafter, hardly a year after we came back to Germany we received news of his death. I was so grateful to God for the opportunity to make up with him before he expired. After he died he appeared to me in the dream. I saw him on the opposite side of the street where I stood looking at me as though he regretted the misunderstanding we had, leaving me with the impression he was unhappy. Thereafter, I said the Divine Mercy prayer for him.

He was Catholic. Thereafter, I dreamt of him again but this time he talked happily with me on the phone, expressing joy over the news of our visit, so I knew he was alright. The Divine Mercy prayer is a very powerful prayer and I'm happy, out of God's Mercy, to be of help. It is indeed very essential to have a forgiving and a merciful heart.

Everything that has a beginning has an end. In December 2008, during my visit to Nigeria, I met a young pastor, he deviated from the Catholic Church to join the Assembles of God's mission, who used to visit my family to pray for Antonia. Then I had no idea he had a Catholic background. This he revealed to me later, on phone, when I tried to inform him of the beauty of the Catholic Church after my return back to Germany. However, in course of time I felt the pastor would not have left the Catholic Church if indeed his gift of clairvoyance was of God. Jesus is the Truth, the Light and the Life so, His Word abides forever.

If He said He will be with His Church until the end of the world, that the gate of hell will not prevail against her, I saw no reason for Him to grant such Grace to someone who is in His Holy Church only for such a one to desert His Church, instead of using the Gift of the Holy Spirit bestowed on him to edify the Holy Church of God. It did not make sense to me. God is not a God of confusion. However, Jesus goes to any length for the salvation of humanity, for any of His lost sheep. He gives everyone equal opportunity to accept or reject Him. In order to save me from the grasp of Satan He did not hesitate to use his means to pull me out. Nevertheless, on seeing Anthony's picture at my parents' residence this young pastor called him immediately a wicked man.

This pastor, in his late twenties then, made me understand Anthony committed many crimes having sold his soul to the devil. "He must confess his crimes and repent or he would go to hell" the pastor continued. He revealed to me Anthony was an agent of evil spirits. He received his prayer from the cemetery and possessed the ability to leave his body to commit evil. "The instrument of darkness tell us truths, win us with honest trifles to betray in deepest consequence" Perhaps, Satan intended to pull me more into his den through this pastor who aimed at using me to come to Germany where he knew nobody. That would have subjected me to caring for him until he could be on his feet. He would have been another Anthony, using the same trick of receiving messages from God to hold me hostage. How could people dare use God's Name in vain! However, all of a sudden everything took shape and I could understand Anthony's queer character, his persistence in trying to make me believe people could leave their body and make astral travel. I then understood the reason of the nature of his conversation, completely out of the ordinary, always about the devil and evil spirits. There was nothing lively about him except, of course, when he was the center of attraction, performing as a clown and demonstrating his magical tricks. He made unfruitful attempts to convince me one does not need Jesus but God. How could that be, I thought, when the Bible stated clearly one must acknowledge that Jesus came in the flesh. Whatever Anthony intended to achieve with that I would not know, as I did not fall for it.

Nevertheless, it did not matter to me whether the pastor was true or false, the important thing to me was the fact he knew things I never revealed to any one for the fear of going insane. Anthony himself informed me, with his own lips, he went to the cemetery, after putting a basin of water in the middle of his room and put a lighted candle in the middle of it. According to him, he set out at mid-night without looking back, as he was instructed. He was not supposed to forget the route he took, therefore, he marked it, as it was total darkness, otherwise, he would not have been able to trace his way back to his home and that would have meant his death. Many have died being unable to trace their way back he informed me. Most important was the secret word which he was not supposed to forget, if he did, it would also have spelt his death. No one else was supposed to know about such things, he said.

Having been strictly warned I never dared reveal it to my father. That was a very big mistake on my part, had I informed him I would have been less troubled. Besides, Anthony made me to understand, it was indeed the way to receive supernatural gifts from God. The eeriness of it all, made me accept everything he told me in good faith. Anyway, the pastor knew what he said otherwise, he would not have hit the nail on the head. My task was to inform Anthony to make his confession. When I informed him he said he would not make any confession, if he did he would be killed for revealing their secret, should I reveal it he would deny it. With that I felt I have done what I was supposed to do. One can take a horse to water but one cannot force it to drink. I have always accused Anthony of not acting like a Christian and now I knew my accusation was not wrong and realized how naive I have been all these years and wasted my youth for nothing. He had so much attachment to the promises made to him by the powers of darkness. Such promises he had a life span of over hundred years, promises I took to be from God, how wrong I realized I was. The promise he would be a rich man, resulted to his pursuit of wealth that led to gambling making him as poor as a church mouse.

Having now being confronted with reality, I began, as though through a magnifying glass, to see his true character and realized I never knew him. Thereafter, I began to distance myself from him as I did not want to have anything to do with the evil he embodied. The more I distanced myself from him the more he pursued me with his evil means. My dreams became nightmares. Sometimes I would be pursued in Cathedrals by some dark horrible beings. He always threatened, in the attempt to scare me, it did not matter where one would be one would always be reached. I did not give thought to it at the time, knowing how he always talked, thinking he was only being mouthy as usual. However, the more he pursued me in my dreams the more I engaged myself in prayer. Although, then I never thought the dreams had anything to do with him, despite the fact I was sleeping in the same room with him, but separately. I could not cope with sleeping together with him any longer, having been humiliated and insulted several times, throwing all my efforts to help him to the dogs. He welcomed my refusal to sleep with him on the same bed with disgust. It would have boosted his ego if I had continued to tolerate and allowed myself his continual insolence and humiliation, to his pleasure.

Fortunately for me, before I travelled to Nigeria in 2008 I had the opportunity to hear, for the first time, the Divine Mercy prayer sung on EWTN and I was so deeply touched that tears rolled down my cheeks. To offer to the Almighty Father the Body, Blood, Soul and Divinity of His dearly Beloved Son roused such emotion in me that gave me an insight of the awful grief in the Heart of the Almighty Father, holding the corpse of His only Beloved Son, who He offered for me, in His Arms. I realized how deeply, infinitely God loves me and such an infinite love deserves to be reciprocated and nourished. I quickly learnt to say the prayer and it became one of my favorite prayers. I believe it was God's Mercy for me to discover the prayer when I did and I have received much Graces from it.

VII. Overcoming

Now together with Grace, Antonia's daughter, then aged four, who was living with me, I began saying family Rosary in the living room, where Anthony stayed and slept, hoping he would join us, but he never did. He would either sleep or disturb the prayer. Realizing he had no interest whatsoever, we began praying elsewhere without him. However, I felt sorry for my blindness all the years unable to realize if he were Christian, as he claimed to be, endowed with such a gift as his prayer, he would have delightfully encouraged family prayer which would have helped the children grow up to be good Catholic Christians. Instead he made life a hell for them and ruined their childhood. His disinterest in the Rosary was a puzzle to me as I hoped for his recovery through prayer. At this time he had ousted my sons out of the home with his problems leaving me and Grace who came to stay with us in 2001, then four years old, alone with him.

It was after my return from Nigeria in 2008, having become aware he was an agent of evil spirits and confronted him with it, I began having nightmares in my dreams, having challenged him openly, about his evil deeds and made known to him the revelations of the pastor in Nigeria, informing him of his fate should he fail to receive the sacrament of reconciliation, I realized the reason for his disinterest in the Rosary as it is a sure weapon against Satan and he was his agent. The Rosary is the contemplation of the life of Jesus Christ through the eyes of His Mother. What a weapon!

Rather than repenting, Anthony became more wicked, threatening to get me and Grace out of the apartment. He had no need of me anymore, someone else should take care of him. He needed a woman help who would live with him therefore, Grace and I should move out of the apartment for her. I had no intension of moving out of the apartment besides, it was not easy to find one and if at all the rent would be exorbitant. Had it not been for the Mercy of God, there was no way I could have tolerated another woman of his choice sharing the apartment with us. One can simply imagine what a hell that would have been for me considering his attitude and his dirty language. However, his much trouble and agitation led to the court finding him someone else, having given to the representative of the court who came on routine visit for him, the impression he needed another care. From then on I was relieved of the burden of being responsible for him. Little did I know it was to my advantage, the beginning of my liberation from his tyranny. However, he could not hide his joy the court gave him a female lawyer, with his sharp tongue, although his delight was short lived when he discovered, to his amazement and disappointment, the female Lawyer was not for letter-writing.

As for me having been relieved from his care, his constant threat of chasing me out of the apartment instigated me, despite the high price, to search for another one with the hope of getting one before the arrival of my mother and immediate younger sister Ifeoma who were due to come in summer of 2009. As God would have it, my application to the housing authority was successful and I was issued with an emergency certificate for an apartment with three rooms and a living room suitable for disabled. This was the only means to get a social apartment with tolerant rent. When God stretches out a helping Hand He never withdraws it until He finishes His mission. Fortunately, having procured the emergency certificate, the housing authority was later informed Anthony was not moving out with us so his name was cancelled. But to my utter surprise, none of the apartments offered me was to my taste therefore, my only alternative was to remain in the apartment with Anthony, and continue to bear his insolence and abuses watching my fate.

But somehow, thereafter it was suddenly called to my mind, the dream I had in which I saw my father and Jesus Christ descending from the sky together, low enough for me to recognize them. My father then came down, while Jesus watched him sit down on a chair in the balcony. He did not enter the apartment. Then it dawned on me I was actually not meant to move away from the flat. Jesus, my real Father and God, was watching over me and asked my father to remain there in the balcony to stop me from moving out. On remembering this dream, I knew Anthony was the one to move out, but how? I needed to have patience. I must wait on the Lord.

The summer of 2009 came, my mother and my sister Ifeoma arrived to witness the horror that was my cup of tea. Anthony, who had no respect for any one, not even for my mother, became more wild than ever, threatening to call the police to send my mother and sister out of the flat. In order to stop me from using the telephone in the room he seized it with the notion it belonged to him, preventing me from contacting anyone. My sympathy was for my mother who was on medical visit witnessing the mess of my life which until now I hid from her. Watching the misery of a loved one and unable to help is very heart-rending. Such was the condition of my mother who was not used to much words, listening to Anthony's dirty language. However, we were left with the only weapon of every Christian, prayer. We sang praises to the Holy Name of God and worshiped Him. For seven days we were in mid-night prayer seeking God's Mercy and protection. After the mid-night prayer we were confident God will surely find a solution to the problem and our wonderful God did. Our good God answers prayers if we trust in Him.

Anthony himself paved way for the solution. He carried out his threat of calling the police telling them lies on the phone about me and my mother and sister, pretending to be crying, as though he was afraid of us. Therefore, on hearing his conversation with the police, I asked for the receiver which, surprisingly he gave me, probably banking on his disability and confident the police have bought the lies he told them. Thereafter, I then informed the police of his tricks and told them he had not yet had his medication. Having heard from me the police did not see any further the need to come.

On another occasion, in his antagonism he scratched me, called the police telling them my mother and sister were strangers he did not want in his apartment. This time the police came, but there was nothing they could do having discovered the strangers in question were actually my mother and sister and so they left, but not without recording the scratch on my hand. Anthony simply was wicked, only peaceful if all danced to his tune as he derived pleasure in the displeasure of those around him. Those he could dominate and make to dance to his tune he tolerated. Nothing is right unless it is done his own way. His intention was to stop any relation of mine having contact with me so he could have his way with me. Unfortunately for him I did not buy his prayer anymore which was a torn in my flesh.

The last straw that broke the camel's back and opened a window for me was the day Anthony grew so furious over nothing. He became so wild due to my refusal to open the bedroom door where I slept in the attempt to avoid his problem. In his state of vehement anger he smashed the door, pulled the telephone away from the socket and carried it to the living room where he occupied. This time the police became aware he was becoming uncomfortable to live with, so with the help of the female lawyer, his help, he was taken out of the flat into old people's home.

Thereafter, after he left the apartment he began terrorizing me with diabolical means. It was a very trying time for me. I had no one with whom I could discuss about it. My mother and sister had flown back to Nigeria and I was left alone to face the unseen enemy. This time I was being attacked both in dreams and awake. Once, I woke up in the dream, to see him put a snake on the bed while Emmanuel, my elder son, and I were asleep. He stood watching to see the snake bite us. Fortunately, having seen it, I prevented it from biting us by directing it away from us and it crawled away. Another occasion the light in the room was shaking together with the shadow of the light on the wall. Had it not been for my belief in God I would not have been able to sleep in the apartment any more out of fear. When he pulled at my eiderdown while I was half asleep I knew what was going on, it was the enemy, Anthony, and kicked at the unseen enemy to show I was not afraid of it. Having done that it became furious and bounced on me trying to strangle me. The only thing I could say was "My Lord Jesus Christ where are you?" and in that very instant it left me.

The Lord has been merciful unto me a miserable sinner. I cannot thank the Lord enough for all His benefits. It is always very beneficial to take shelter in God and be permanently under His Protection by doing His Holy Will so that His most Precious Blood will always cover and protect us. It is sometimes difficult for one to believe certain things do happen because one have not had personal experience of them, but that does not rule out the fact that such things exist, evil exists. It is wise therefore, to learn from the experience of another rather than wait for personal experience.

When Jesus says the devil exists, then he exists. If He says there is hell, then there is hell. Jesus is the Truth He can neither deceive nor be deceived. Humanity is indeed blessed to have won God's Love. This Love is a priceless Treasure, infinite Protection against all evil, the ultimate Eternal Joy in Heaven for everyone who has learnt to cherish and nourish it. There are agents of Satan all over the world who move about in sheep's clothing. The only protection against evil is our faith in God, trust in Jesus Christ who defeated the powers of darkness. It is essential to avoid sin. It is Satan's means of reaching God's children. Sin separates the soul from God. God hates sin. He who is not in a state of Grace is food for Satan, he throws himself at the folly of Satan, separates himself from God's protection.

Now that Anthony was out of the apartment, arrangement was made for Antonia who was sent to Nigeria by Anthony to my family, after misusing her in the pretense to make her his biological child as he was instructed by his prayer, to come back to Germany. I wondered why he did not send her to his own family after he caused her insanity. However, she was then under the care of my younger sister Ifeoma, without any financial assistance from Anthony. The care for my aged mother coupled with her care due to her mental instability became burdensome for Ifeoma, now a widow. Therefore, it was decided she should come to me as the mother. My eagerness to have her back, after such a long separation, coupled with the hope she would be completely healed, through prayer if she stayed with me, led to her arrival in summer 2010 in the company of Ifeoma and my mother who was on her medical visit. My mother's medical visits were sponsored by my younger brothers, Lawrence and Matthew Jr. It was a great joy feeling the Lord has joined my daughter to her brothers and my family which was scattered was now complete. How wrong I was!

At first everything seemed peaceful and harmonious until my mother and Ifeoma travelled back to Nigeria. In order to be in the company of Catholic Christians to avoid lonesomeness, God helped me become a member of CFC, couples for Christ through Gloria, an acquaintance from the Philippines. In December 2010, during the general assembly, I was in attendance with Antonia and Grace her daughter together with Jenne, the acquaintance from Cameroun married to a Ghanaian. Being concerned about Antonia's health I objected to her drinking wine, as it contained alcohol, due to the medications she took for her mental health, as bread and wine was being served. To my utter surprise I was met with such hostility which I never thought was possible from her. All of a sudden she was out of her mind insulting and abusing me, shouting at me. I was embarrassed and dumbfounded. I could not believe my ears hearing all the insolence coming from the daughter I loved. In an attempt to calm her down and pull her down to earth I threatened she would not drive home with us in her state. I had expected an apology, but instead she became more furious, wilder and louder asking me to call the police. Her reason for the police I did not know then.

However, Jenne was able to calm her down making her realize her wrong which consequently led to her apology and we drove home. This was the beginning of a series of manifestation of Antonia's true character. On many occasions, during her stay in Nigeria, Ifeoma informed me of her wickedness, but I never believed it, due to Antonia's good nature before her ailment. Had it not been God's Grace I would not have had the face to attend the CFC meetings again, considering the humiliation she caused me. Despite the cold reception from some members who were, prior to this incidence friendly, I kept my cool without bothering what they thought of me, but with time, the Lord vindicated me, cleared my face and everyone became aware of the truth after my testimony of God's goodness to me.

Nevertheless, on Christmas day that same year 2010 Antonia almost ruined our Christmas had I not determined not to let that happen. This time the problem was between her and her daughter Grace. Antonia needed an English German dictionary from her daughter who could not find where she kept it. Disbelieving her daughter she gave her a thorough beating whereby she broke her daughter's little finger. During their quarrel I was in prayer in my chapel. At the time my prayer was finished, on hearing the sound of their quarrel I rushed out to intervene and received two blows from Antonia on my breast. This instigated me to call the police as I could not control her. All her efforts to deceive the police, pretending she was a quiet and well-behaved girl, could not help her as I made it clear to the police she was a green snake in a green grass. Fortunately, the letter for her care came from the court the previous day authorizing me to be her "care' which enabled the police take her to the hospital for mentally retarded where she spent two months.

My sons who usually came over to me on Christmas-eve could not make it this time due to the problem of Antonia. On their arrival, seeing the Police vehicles, the ambulance, parking before the house, they went home believing it was Antonia's problem. How right they were. They did not want to get involved due to the police besides, there was nothing they could have done and I was glad they went home to avoid spoiling Christmas-eve for my grandson, Junior who was then nine months old, Emmanuel's son with his German Yugoslavian wife, Tamara. Thereafter, after Antonia was admitted into the hospital Grace and I returned home to make the best of the Christmas-eve as we could.

All things work out for good to them that love God. This incidence induced me reject being her care so a lady lawyer was assigned to her. My intention was for her to go from the hospital to a home for mentally retarded, but her "care" decided she should come home to me, after her discharge, until she found a home for her. It was a decision that met with my resentment, yet I decided to cope with it in good faith, which, on the long run, turned out to be a blessing in disguise. I could not understand the reason for Antonia's insubordination, her rudeness and insolence after all the efforts I made for her comfort. I forgave her whole-heartedly the disgrace at the CFC meeting. It never affected my relationship with her. But somehow, I gradually began to discover she knew exactly what she was doing and enjoyed doing it. Her capability to reason logically and sensibly was amazing just as her animosity was baffling.On the long run, in my confusion, I began to realize she was in love with Anthony who she called papa, although she knew very well he was not her father. How could she be in love with the man who misused her I wondered. In love with an agent of the evil spirit? Who was responsible for her ailment, how could she even think of it. It was difficult to believe, but it is true.

I had hoped she would join me in prayer for the liberation of us all from Anthony's damonic activities. I was mistaken. The agent of Satan embeded his wickedness deep into her which she accepted on her own free will. Now I realized the reason for her outburst at the CFC, an attempt to keep me away from the group where I had contact with the word of God, a place where I was in the midst of those who strive in prayer, to make it easier for him to reach me. He wickedly turned my own daughter, with demonic means, against me. Fortunately, his plan to eject me out of the CFC group was a failure. Although Antonia's attachment to Anthony was a shocking surprise, Providence smiled at me.

My problem now became how to convince my sons Anthony used evil spirits to influence their behavior. Until now it has not been easy for me but I have left everything in the Hands of God who will surely vindicate me at His own time. God has been merciful to me a sinner. Our good God granted me the Grace to dream dreams which relate to reality. This way He kept me aware of Anthony's activities with his diabolical means. Once I dreamt of him trying to enter into my apartment, looking like an insane man. I refused him entry and asked the neighbors to call the police. Suddenly, in the same dream I saw him in a pit with Grace. I immediately put my sons, Emmanuel and Peter in the car to keep them away from Anthony. With difficulty I managed to pull Grace out of the pit away from him into the car and drove away with her and the boys. It was surprising Antonia was not in the dream. However, I gave no thought to it, but informed Grace of the dream to make her aware of what we had to deal with in order for her to think and act as a Christian girl and be prayerful. This was because I observed she had two personalities which was frighteningly disturbing.

Sometimes she would be such a sweet girl every mother would love to have, sometimes one could hardly recognize her. She would flare up with such furious anger, her body and lips shaking as though she was possessed. All that mattered to her in such moments was herself, using insulting tone and bad language which otherwise was strange to her, but somehow I did not fail to realize the resemblance to Anthony and

Antonia with their sharp insulting tongues. Had God not granted me wisdom she would have been a threat to herself, I thought then. The only way to pull her down to earth, with difficulty, was to give her a spank. I despised it, but there was no other alternative as I did not want her to take my silence as weakness and grow wings.

Nevertheless, on that same day, before dawn, about three-forty a.m. I woke up to ease myself and saw light in Antonia's room. Without hesitation I went to her room thinking she might be sleeping without turning off the light or watching obscene films shown late at night on Television as usual. I strictly warned her from watching such films. To my utter surprise, on opening her door she rushed to it with such velocity and aggression to close the door with force, but realizing there was no key to it she picked up her dirty tight stained with her mensuration and spanked me on the shoulder with it. Thereafter, in the attempt to make her realize what she did I picked it up and spanked her back with it. That was putting petrol into the fire. This time she spanked me with it on the face, abused me telling me off at the same time. Her angry abusive voice woke up Grace who rushed to the room and witnessed, as she spanked me with her milky colored tight, stained all over with blood, and gave an exclamation of surprise. I stood there in disgust beholding the person I could not believe I carried for nine months in my womb. However, I was grateful to God for the Grace to take it all with humility. I sent Grace to bed, went also to bed under the protection of the Almighty Father.

However, at breakfast, same day, she apologized, although aware it was not genuine, I informed her I had already forgiven her before she asked for it. I really did forgive her as my forgiving her had nothing to do with her apology. I forgive everyone who offends me, even if they did not apologize but I do not condone evil. Thereafter, she continued with her rudeness threatening she would turn against me and say I asked Anthony to misuse her. What a shock it was as I sadly realized I was harboring an enemy in disguise. However, I made it clear to her she would not be believed. She had already given the right statement at the hospital when it all happened, with her lips. Although she withdrew it later, out of sympathy for Anthony, I informed her the record would still be there in the achieve. On Grace question why she did not reveal it to her aunty Ifeoma with whom she lived all those years if what she said was true. Her answer was simply "I did not remember" "If you could not remember then, how could you remember now after twenty years?" Grace rejoined, but she gave no reply. However, the fact her record was still in the hospital's achieve silenced her.

Having received so much insolence, false accusation and animosity from her I was left with no alternative than to denounce her as my daughter and made no secret about it. One can forgive someone and yet punish him for his offence. However, she thought it was mere words and attempted, one evening after meal, to give me a good-night kiss which I rejected with an exclamation of resentment and disgust. The falsehood of her gesture was irritating. Afterwards, remembering how much I care about the Lord's feelings, I felt sorry for my action and pondered in my heart, when I woke up from sleep at night, over my action, if I hurt the Lord's feelings, and dosed off again. In my dream I found myself with the family including my second cousin Fidelis. Everyone was there except Antonia. In the room where we were there was a framed picture of a round object with a strange design which had a certain uncomfortable effect on all of us. In order for it to stop affecting us somehow, I found the courage to break the glass. All of a sudden the strange effect it had on us stopped and we felt relief. But when I showed some sign of doubt, wondering whether the strange effect was from the framed picture, it began to affect me again. I then asked the family to pray. They began to say "Blood of Jesus" With difficulty, due to my swollen, heavy cheeks that made it difficult for me to speak I said "No" However, I managed to ask for the Divine Mercy prayer. Immediately the family began to sing the Divine Mercy prayer, at that very moment my swollen, heavy cheek relaxed. We breathed out and began to thank God for His Mercy. It was my first experience of the power of the Divine Mercy prayer.

Suddenly Antonia walked angrily into the room asking to know who spolt her picture and took the damaged framed picture and flunked it out of the window. Surprised at her action," I hope you did not damage my window" was all I could say. Without comment she walked out of the room. When I came outside I saw her sitting beside Anthony who was lying down on the bed. Immediately she saw me she came over to me, grasping my right arm, in pretense to care, she said in a funny voice "Mami" Immediately my arm became heavy, I pushed her away and woke up. When I wake up I still felt the effect of that touch on my arm. I realized this dream was God's revelation to me, I did not hurt His feelings with my decision. It was God's Mercy, I should be aware of Antonia's union with Anthony against me. It was an assurance my decision was right for she was no longer the child I bore as she has turned evil. I was grateful to God for the Grace to let go. At 38 years, knowing good and evil, acting on her own freewill, and as she has chosen evil, I had no choice than to lose myself from her.

Another incidence which proved my decision right and supported my dream was the day I refused her attending Mass with me after she behaved badly. She threatened going mad if she did not go with me and Grace to mass and would destroy everything before we came back. My reply was to assure her of imminent deportation, after spending time in prison, and reminded her of not having visa. However, before Mass, I received the sacrament of penance. In the confessional I informed the priest of my refusal to allow Antonia attend Mass with us. He made me understand it was wrong for everyone must work out his or her own salvation. On that note, without hesitation, not wanting to be an impediment to anyone's salvation, I drove home and picked her up before the Mass started. Although when I arrived home to pick her up I found her quite normal. There was no demolition of furniture as she threatened.

But on realizing I came back merely to pick her up she felt triumphant and began putting up an air of importance.

Thereafter, to my great disgust however, Anthony sneaked under my eiderdown while I was sleeping that night. At dawn, I was very sad and apologetic to my Beloved Jesus who revealed to me already my decision about Antonia was right. The priest had no idea about my dreams therefore, I should have been able to have acted independently being fully aware of my relationship with Jesus. I should not have brought her to Mass. She received the Holy Eucharist unworthily. May the Lord have mercy.

On 26.03.2011, having made it clear to Antonia my intention of not attending Mass with her any more, as I did not want any distractions while receiving Jesus in the Eucharist. I decided to go earlier on this day to enable me spend enough time with Jesus in front of the Tabernacle before the beginning of the Mass. To my utter surprise she was already dressed up to follow me. How she managed to know I was to go earlier was a puzzle to me. Despite her being ready I declined her attempt to follow me but as I was closing the door behind me I overheard her say in vernacular "akatalia n'uka" meaning "will going to Mass prevent it?" On returning from Mass I had the urge to send her back to the hospital as I felt her comment was devilish. That was the last straw that broke the camel's back.

Surprisingly, at the hospital admission was denied her on the ground she was not sick enough to be admitted. Their reason being she was not aggressive and can take care of herself. I was made to understand she was of good disposition, very co-operative and friendly. This was the impression she gave them during her two months admission earlier, at Christmas 2010. For this reason the hospital reduced her medication to one tablet in the morning and one in the evening without any more injections. I was made to understand she would be fine as long as she took her medications as prescribed. Somehow, the hospital's decision did not surprise me at all. I was already aware, due to God's Mercy, she knew exactly what she was doing, camouflaging her true character before those outside the family. Now being aware of her wickedness I knew I could not possibly be under the same roof with her for long therefore, I took steps to put an end to it. To this end I had her registered in a Catholic hostel for disabled women on waiting list.

As things ran out of control, being unable to cope with her queer behavior I became eager to have her out of my apartment as quickly as possible having become unsure of her next move. As there was no longer any trust, Grace and I began taking precautions for our security by locking the doors of our respective rooms at night while sleeping. Moreover, in order to know when she went to the kitchen in our absence we would place some thread in an unnoticeable manner on the door, should the position change, it would mean she went into the kitchen. This was to enable us then inspect the food items if she tampered with them. The whole situation created the feeling of being in an enemy zone in one's own four walls. After all, one's home should be a place of security and peace in God's love.

On the 28.03.2011, I drove her to the emergency home office in the hope of procuring her with a room to herself from where she would then move into the Catholic home for disabled whenever a room was free for her, as living with her became more burdensome and unsafe. To my disappointment, after her particulars were taken, I was informed a room would be given her, as soon as it was clear how the room would be financed. That threw me into utter confusion, not being financially balanced for it myself. Besides, having arrived Germany with visiting visa it was not easy to obtain residence permit for her therefore, she had no right to social-welfare benefits. It would have been better if she had arrived with a visa for joining her family in Germany. Unfortunately there was no room to wait for the process as she was to arrive in the company of my mother and sister.

However, shortly after we arrived home she confronted me with the request to take her to her father, meaning Anthony, who was in a disabled home. That was an opportunity, I thought, to remove her from my home and stop locking everywhere night and day. But before taking her to Anthony I must inform my elder son Emmanuel, as I had much respect for his feelings. Fortunately, I could neither reach him on his land line nor on cell phone for which I was grateful to God. Had I reached him he would have opposed the idea making it difficult for me to act. Ignorantly he showed sympathy for him due to his disablement, without realizing how wicked he was and should not be pitied for he was evil.

Suddenly, Antonia's "care" the lady-lawyer, responsible for her place of stay, who has been impossible to reach on the phone, called. After fruitless efforts I gave up trying to phone her, she neither reacted to the message left on her mail box nor picked her calls. In my desperate situation I decided not to miss the opportunity Antonia herself presented to me, to dump her by Anthony in the hostel but on second thought however, it dawned on me she might be brought back to me if I just dumped her by him without the permission of her "care" I became restless. In my utter confusion and helplessness I rested my head on our Blessed mother, Our Lady of Guadalupe and simply told her she is my Mother and repeated "I'm I not here your Mother?". Hardly did I finish saying this the telephone rang and it was Antonia's "care" who then permitted me to take her to Anthony from where she was taken to a temporary stay with other women in an emergency apartment. That was how I got rid of her. I thanked Our Blessed Mother for her loving motherly care.

Antonia was later granted a room in the Catholic home in which I registered her. She is being well cared for having been born in Germany. For her own benefits, arrangements have been made to get her an identity card for disabled. She is now entitled to social-welfare benefits.

Nevertheless, another astonishing event in this my complicated life took place on 11.04.2011. Suddenly the shadow of the light in my bedroom began shaking as I was about to retire for the night. Remembering it has happened before, I simply ignored it putting my trust in God. As usual, I curdled myself in the Arms of Jesus and slept off. At about 12.30 am I woke up, eased myself, said my prayer as usual and was on the verge of falling asleep, suddenly my bed began to sway to and fro gradually like a swing. At once I knew Anthony was at work, in the attempt to scare me, having promised me it did not matter where I was, I would be reached. Antonia's threat with "akatalia n'uka" actually reminded me of its significance with Anthony's promise but at the time I did not give thought to it. As was already mentioned, after Anthony sold his soul to Satan he could leave his body through astral travel. He made fruitless attempts to draw me into it with his unceasing explanations. For this purpose, he purchased a band of encyclopedia Britannica, on the pretense it was for comparative religion, but the whole lecture usually got me scared to the skin.

However, having ignored the eerie swaying of the bed I felt the eiderdown being pulled, I kicked at it, without seeing what I was kicking at, and pulled my eiderdown upwards towards myself. All of a sudden the unseen attacker gripped my whole body, throwing me into a state of confusion. I remembered the Divine Mercy, but was unable to start it immediately, so I exclaimed "My Lord Jesus Christ where are You?" and in that very instant the unseen attacker left me. St. Paul, the Apostle, rightly said we are fighting with principalities and powers in high places. If one had no experience of such demonic attacks it sounds like fables. The only remedy to it is a close relationship with Jesus who conquered the powers of darkness. He is Almighty. Therefore, a regular attendance of the Holy Mass, resentment of sin, remaining in a state of Grace, receiving the Sacrament of reconciliation, and above all receiving Jesus in the Eucharist are very essential. Jesus is Trustworthy and Faithful.

After this experience, I asked Jesus not to allow such things happen to me again as I belong exclusively to Him. I reminded Him that my body is the Temple of the living God and the Holy Trinity dwells in me. Jesus heard me and such a thing never happened again and never will. I am so unworthy for God's Love. His Love for me overwhelms me. I am an unworthy, wretched miserable nothing, less than half of an Ant, yet He showers me with great Love and affection. I cannot be able to thank Him enough. My life today is a life of gratitude to the Eternal Father for the sacrifice He made of His only Son for the salvation of the world, for me. For the Eternal Father to allow His only begotten Son to undergo such extreme bitter passion, to reconcile me to Himself proves to me He will deny me nothing, as long as it is beneficial to my soul. O, how wonderful it is to have such a wonderful Father! I am very proud of Him.

As was mentioned before, my father was a righteous and devout Christian. He loved Jesus much. Although a non-Catholic Christian, until just before his departure from this terrifying wilderness, He carried his cross triumphantly through the Grace of God. Jesus knows those who are His, those, through no fault of theirs are not in His Holy Church, in the One Holy Catholic and Apostolic Church He built on Peter. The enemy, Satan, used the many waters I went through to try my father. The episode of the priest, the diplomat and Anthony who seduced his granddaughter, dumped her by him to deal with the disgrace of her insanity, coupled with my deprivation from visiting him for twenty-eight years to face the embarrassment of the questioning eyes of his neighbors on the whereabouts of his eldest daughter. Anthony, the priest and the diplomat were all instruments of darkness, of the enemy to shake my father's Faith, but God never abandons His own. I am grateful to God he went home as Catholic and is in Heaven. That He departed as Catholic was confirmed by a Catholic Priest during my visit to Nigeria in 2008. He informed me my father's acceptance to be Catholic, though unable to make it due to circumstances, he went home as Catholic. The Divine clarification of it, later, was his appearance with Jesus, as already mentioned, for my protection.

To be a priest in the One Holy Catholic and Apostolic Church founded by Jesus is a privilege that must be honored, cherished, respected and appreciated by every Catholic Priest. The abuse of Priesthood is an insolence to the person of Jesus Christ, a slap and a spit on His Face, an ingratitude to the Father's Divine Mercy. Most people would be disappointed in the end if they took God's Mercy for granted. Nevertheless, that some Priests abuse the Priesthood is not a guarantee for any one misused by the priest to condemn the Church. The Church is not responsible for the sin of the Priest. The priest himself is responsible for his sins. To criticize the Church is to criticize Jesus. The Church is His Body for which He shed His Most Precious Blood. The Church is Holy, though the members are sinful, because the Founder, Jesus Christ, is Holy. Jesus came to seek and find what was lost therefore, He is aware the members are sinful. "If anyone has no sin let him throw the first stone." Besides, it is His desire to allow the weeds grow with the wheat until the time of Harvest when the Angels will do the harvesting. The weeds, He said, were planted by the enemy. One should pray for the priests and let family matters remain within the family. The Church is the Family of God whose Head Jesus Christ is, He is able to manage His Church. He is her jurisdiction.

For the sanctification of the Church Jesus adorned Her with seven Sacraments among which the Sacrament of Reconciliation is a source of drawing Divine Mercy. The Church does not need any stimuli, any worldly organization or government, to interfere in the affairs of the Church. The government of this world and the One, Holy, Catholic and Apostolic Church of Jesus Christ are two autonomous Bodies. They have nothing in common. The Catholic Church is Divine, She possesses Divine guidance. Her one and only Judge is Jesus Christ Himself, therefore, anyone who condemns the Church of God should be careful lest he be in danger of fighting against the Almighty God.

Of course it is a mortal sin, a disgrace, a spit on the face of Jesus Christ, for a Priest to abuse the Priesthood by misusing the little ones in his care. If the Pope, the Vicar of Christ, utilizes the Sacrament of Reconciliation what stops a Priest from doing so regularly, being aware of the enemy at his heels. The Priesthood is a sacred vocation and not a profession, therefore, a Priest should be an example to the observation of the commandments of God, faithful to his priestly vows. No one should enter the Priesthood without a thorough examination of conscience, to be confident it is his vocation. A Priest must bear on mind the priestly vocation is a commitment to Jesus Christ. He must, for his priestly vocation detach himself from worldly desires, goods and pleasures for a reward in Heaven. A priest should remain in Constant communion with his Divine Master, nurture devotion to our Lady, saying the Rosary, receive the Sacrament of Reconciliation frequently. Holy Hours are very essential for a fulfilled Priestly vocation. A battle known is half won therefore, being aware of the existence of Satan and his evil intentions is enough reason for every child of God, especially the Priests, to put on the amour of God, prayer.

A Cardinal Schönborn once said he asked Jesus how He was able to remain celebrate during His earthly life, being truly human with so much compassion, yet, was able to put flesh under subjection, and received no written answer. This was in his address to some youthful audience in his topic on establishing a personal relationship with Jesus. Jesus does not need to give a written answer to such a question because the answer is obvious. It is Love. The Will to please the Beloved leaves no room for other matters. The focus on the goal becomes pre-eminent. He kept His focus on accomplishing the Father's Will. Love guarantees total awareness of what is at stake should one lose focus. In order not to lose focus Jesus kept constant contact with His Father in prayer. This resulted in the ultimate decision of carrying out the Father's Will till its bitter end, despite His agony in the garden of olives. Besides, He was aware why the Word took flesh, to redeem the world, to seek and find what was lost, the Lamb must be spotless. The love for the Eternal Father called for obedience, the focus on the objective therefore, Love is the answer to everything. It leaves no room for trifle. It is an indissoluble bond, selfless, sacrificial even unto death. Jesus is an example for His Priests.

Jesus said "....whosoever causes one of these little ones who believe in me to sin, it would be better for him if a great millstone were hung round his neck and he were thrown into the sea" Mk 9 vs 42. God is the Judge and I bet you He knows exactly what to do. Concerning the unfortunate ones who fell prey to Priests with depraved minds, it is not advisable to criticize the Church which is the mystical Body of Jesus and give room to the enemy, Satan, to blind you and lead you astray, depriving you from working out your salvation which Jesus bought for you with a bitter price. Besides, love bears all things, if you have a genuine love for God then allow Him to console you while you console Him in return for the agony in His Sacred Heart. It is out of place to take what belongs to the family to the enemy, to the world, for this is exactly the motive of Satan, to discredit the Church by means of Priests with depraved minds, who have allowed themselves to be his instruments to hurt their Divine Master who loves them infinitely. A priest who falls away woefully, knowing the truth possesses a sick soul and needs to be pitied.

There is a priest I happened to hear about who deserted the Church, his Bridegroom, for the lust of the flesh and got married. Although this priest, fully aware a priest, after ordination, cannot marry again, yet still acts as a priest, conferring the sacraments of the Church to members of his church as a Catholic priest. His problem is selfishness and ego. He cannot prove to be ignorant of his insubordination to the Pope and that he is acting against the Holy Will of God. One cannot help but believe he delights in providing food for the media which is always on the hunt for means to discredit the One, Holy, Catholic and Apostolic Church of the Most High God. Such priests acting against the Holy Will of Jesus Christ do they think they are serving Him? How could such priests ever think they would be pleasing Him. They are nothing but mere instruments of Satan to discredit the Holy Church of Jesus Christ, deceiving the children of God. No one can impose his own will on God and claim to serve Him. Any one whose focus is Heaven must comply to the Holy Will of God. Our good Lord made it clear that blind leaders leading the blind both fall into the pit. Therefore, it is wise for those who run after such blind leaders, priests in sheep's clothing, to think twice before they leap.

Moreover, I would suggest those misused or mislead by such priests should rather take me for an example, having been misled by a priest also. Although I was then not Catholic, but today a passionate Catholic, having Jesus as my best Friend. Jesus healed my wounds. He will heal yours if you permit Him. Your predicament should draw you more closer to Him who loves you infinitely and understands you beyond your imagination. Rather than fall into self-pity, have compassion for Jesus, our Beloved Redeemer, Who is suffering from unrequited love of His Beloved Children. He shed His most precious Blood to found His Church, established the Priesthood in order not to leave us as orphans, yet some of His Priests stain the Priesthood. Think of Him, for love of you He became a prisoner in our Tabernacles. Be subdued in humble trust by the Merciful Love of the God Who died the painful death on the Cross for love of you. It would be to your benefit if you established a personal relationship with Him. I would suggest you give Him your heart, accept His, and experience love in your being as you never dreamt of for He is Love. He will help you know the meaning of love and you would find profound peace and equilibrium, hence your future lies in His Hands.

However, in order to end the chapter of Anthony in my life, in God's infinite Mercy, his deceased father appeared to me in the dream. I got to know him when he came on visit. I informed him about my intention to separate from his son who deceived me with letters from evil spirits which consequently compelled me to a union with him.

I made it clear to him that for this great deceit no marriage existed between us. He showed no surprise. His nonchalant acceptance of my intention gave me the impression he had knowledge of his son's alliance with Satan. Nevertheless, this did not surprise me anyway, remembering Anthony informed me his father was a member of "ogboni" society, a secret society in Nigeria. Marriage is based on truth, love and mutual understanding, not on deceit. God is Truth and anything otherwise, despite the vows, makes the marriage void. Light and darkness have nothing in common and man cannot serve God and Marmon, hence he sold his soul to Satan for worldly riches which would eventually be destroyed by fire. God does not join Truth and falsehood together. He knows the secrets of the heart. He never abandons those who put their trust in Him. Whenever the time is ripe He extends His saving Hand.

Actually, there is nothing more peaceful and gratifying as total surrender to the Almighty Father. Having developed absolute trust in God provides room for Him to take care of me and mine and of all my affairs. Due to God's infinite Goodness His infinite Love and Care accompanied me on my flight to Nigeria and throughout my stay there in 2011. Being aware I am the Child of the Eternal Father set me free from worries. He bears it all for me for He is such a wonderful Father that would do anything for His Children. All He asks for is "BE THE CHILD I CREATED YOU TO BE AND LEAVE IT ALL TO ME" Trust! Thanks to God, I have absolute Trust in Him.

Well, on the Eve of my flight I planned to check-in my luggage at the airport, but according to the weather-forecast that day was to be wet and snowy. It was the middle of December. I had to inform God the way a child informs his father when he needed something. Having won for myself, from God the Father, the confidence of total reliance on Him like a baby in its mother's arms it became the most natural thing for me to do. On that day it was raining, but as I was to go the rain stopped, there was no snow, my luggage and myself did not get wet. Perhaps, you can imagine the joy in my heart and how proud I was of God. I was over-joyed, like a child who found what his father did extraordinary and overwhelming. At the Airport, as my luggage was to be checked-in it was discovered they were overweight, two boxes, one large and the other middle sized. I was not at all surprised because I knew my luggage was overweight. As I needed everything in them I asked God to ask His Angels to weigh them for me. When the boxes were weighed at home the large one was 29 kg while the middle one weighed 24 kg. But at the Airport, during the checking-in the large one weighed 26 kg instead of 29 kg. I was made to reduce the weight to 23kg which I did by simply removing the pampers that were meant for my aged mother which weighed 3 kg and it was checked in leaving the middle box with 24 kg. To my utter surprise, when it was weighed, it weighed only 4 kg. and was also checked-in. I was out of myself with joy. Again I was full of admiration for my sweet Beloved Heavenly Father. It feels so good having a Father who is Almighty, All Powerful, All Good and All Loving who owns everything and what He wills is.

On the following day, the day of my flight, I went by taxi to the Airport carrying five hand luggage and feeling quite care-free without realizing I would not be allowed to travel with all the hand luggage, until the taxi-driver drew my attention to it on reaching the Airport. He volunteered to assist me with the checking-in but when I informed him my luggage was already checked-in the previous day he exclaimed, informing me I would not be allowed to carry the whole as hand luggage. I simply calmed him down asking him not to mind I was not travelling alone but with Jesus.

All through the drive to the Airport I chatted with him about Jesus, the only conversation I know. Certainly I must have made a good impression on him, with my one and only Love, just as it pleased God, because talking about Jesus fills my heart with great joy that made him offer to help me check-in. I am in my best element talking about my wonderful Savior and Beloved. Nevertheless, on the long run, I was allowed to carry all the five items whereas only 8kg was allowed. Again it did not surprise me, due to the awareness my Eternal Father, whom I adore, whose Merciful Love I realize and appreciate, takes care of me and mine and of all my affaires. I am absolute confident my most Merciful Savior and Beloved, our Lord Jesus Christ will never disappoint, abandon nor deceive me. O how I thank Him for the Grace to believe! Well, one of the hand luggage was the pampers, for my aged mother.

The reason I carried the pampas with me was a certain urge within me to do so as I was about to leave the apartment. God is Almighty, He created and controls the universe. All He requires is that He should be trusted. O yes, one can call it blind trust – yes blind trust! I trust in Him blindly. I have united my will with His. One who loves me so infinitely wants only my good. My will does not matter anymore. This enables me experience Heaven right away in this transitory world. Jesus is Heaven. I pray for the Grace to persevere. Jesus is my world, my Hope, my Life, my only Love, the King of my heart, the Lover of my soul, my Heaven and my sweet All and All.

Now having been allowed to carry all the hand luggage, hardly did I realize how burdensome the luggage would be for me on landing in Frankfurt, on transit. It was then I began to feel the weight of the luggage while searching for the gate leading to the flight for Lagos. Almost on the verge of despair, I wished I carried less luggage, as I hoped to be able to reach the gate on time to catch the flight. Then I sought for my only Help Who is always Faithful and Trustworthy, the Almighty God, in whom there is no disappointment, and asked Him to help me carry them. And guess what? He did. I felt so proud of Him, so proud of my sweet Beloved Heavenly Father who instantly responded to assist His little girl. Not only was the flight delayed, it was announced all passengers to Lagos should check-in their hand luggage free of charge.

Could you imagine that! Without paying a cent for over-weight. That was fantastic, a great relief for me.

> O most merciful Father, infinite Goodness, the best Father,
> The only one God, the only Good God, All Powerful God,
> Creator of Heaven and Earth, Author and Giver of Life. You
> hold the world in Your Hands, from You all things come. Alfa
> and Omega, sweet Beloved Heavenly Father, how happy and
> fortunate I am You are my Father. Your Love overwhelms me.
>
> I am very proud of You and my heart rejoices in You.
> Thank You so much Father for the Grace to know my identity.
> I came from You Father Who created me with love, for love,
> sent me here to know you, serve you and return to be with
> You forever, eternally in Heaven. O Heaven, my eternal Home,
> sweet Home of the Almighty God, my Father, I long for You.
>
> Grant, O sweet Beloved Father that I may always please you.
> Be always merciful unto me, a miserable sinner and love me.
> Grant that I be always worthy of your love for me, that my life be
> a reflection of the Holy Trinity, my God, whom I adore, in Jesus
> Christ, my Love, so that when you call me Home I may come
> straight Home to you in Heaven to rest on your most wonderful,
> most beautiful, most loving fatherly Bosom, O my Dad, my Hero.
>
> To be pampered by you my wonderful Dad, with your fatherly love.
> That I may love you as your darling daughter, praise and worship you
> eternally with your Holy Angels and Saints throughout Eternity. O
> how I look forward to it. Grant me this Grace, dearest Father, through
> Jesus Christ our Lord on whose victorious Cross I have crucified
> self, and offered it to Him, in deepest humility, without reserve – Amen.

Having arrived for Christmas in Nigeria we all travelled to the village to spend the Christmas celebration there. My mother Flora, my sister Ifeoma and her children, Lawrence from the United States and a number of cousins also from the United States together with their mother including a number of other family members were all there. It was a happy reunion and a thing of joy seeing most of my kid relations who have now grown into maturity and some with their own respective families. But in the midst of this great joy Satan played a foul play on me through his agent, Emeka, the husband of my second younger sister Eugenia. I have been informed of his evil activities and this is well known by the family, even my dad whose Faith was being tried. The only one who does not know is Eugenia for fear she may not be able to bear it. It is known in the family Emeka has tried to get rid of her through diabolical means, but due to the Faith of my father in God she is being protected by God through prayer. Besides, any further attempt of Emeka to use diabolical means on her or on any member of the family will send him earlier to his master Satan. The watchful fatherly eyes of the Almighty God is on the family. Having been occupied with my own problems I did not pay much attention to his evil inclinations. However, with God's deliverance and Mercy it was made known to me he is actually an agent of Satan. I dreamt he was sitting alone in an empty room without furniture except the chair on which he sat. The doors and windows were thrown open, the wind blowing and swaying the long white curtains here and there.

I was in search of my mother and came in there hoping to see her. Instead of my mother I saw him alone in the empty room. On seeing him in such an eerie situation I did not know what to make out of it. I could not even inquire about the furniture, but asked him if he saw my mother, he said he did. Thereafter, he gave me wrong direction. My instinct told me my mother would not possibly be where he directed me, so I went to my aunty Pat and found her there. That dream gave me an insight of his mischievousness and evil inclination confirming what was said of him. Constant prayer makes one in tune with God. He begins to make Himself known. He takes away fear. One becomes courageous and Satan is disappointed. The more one prays the more prayer becomes part of one. Prayer is talking with the Father.

As events would have it, during our stay in the village Emeka came to visit with Eugenia. When he saw me he did not greet me. My spirit was moved, instigating me to give him an indirect challenge, referring to all the agents of evil spirits warning that failure to renounce the evil spirits and follow God they will all burn in hell, which is their rightful place having chosen to serve Satan willfully. I made no secret about my love for Jesus emphasizing how I love what He loves and hate what He hates. He became uncomfortable, got up from his chair and moved away in pretense to talk to someone. Thereafter, he accused me of talking to him to which I responded I spoke in general, after all he was not the only one in the room. My mother, my sisters and some few other people were there. Consequently, after they left, Eugenia, my sister, telephoned Ifeoma, who comes before her, informing her of her husband's state of mind. All I know is that the marriage is neither recognized by God nor by me. Darkness and Light has nothing in common. However, I was made to understand Emeka was much displeased with my speech. He did not hesitate, with diabolical means, to make me realize it.

It is said trouble never blows a whistle and wickedness becomes more wicked when exposed. It does not believe in Goodness. After this event we began hearing, every night, the sound of someone walking with walking-stick, on the corridor and inside the house. We took to our weapon, Prayer. My family knows how to pray, so we went deep into it. Thereafter, Holy water was sprinkled everywhere inside the house and invoked as the Blood of Jesus. Although not as Catholics do. The Precious Blood of Jesus is to be honored. My family belongs to Pentecostal Church, but they love God truly. The moment they realize their error of not being in the Holy Church of God they would become Catholics. It is all in the Holy Hand of the Almighty God. It is my prayer. "Be ye one as

I am one with the Father" We have only one God in three persons" Therefore, Jesus desires only one Church and not churches. However, as was earlier indicated, the shouting of "blood of Jesus" "Blood of Jesus" could not help until the Divine Mercy Prayer was said when I was diabolically attacked. Nevertheless, It is true they are not Catholics, yet, God in His infinite Goodness hears the prayers of everyone who seeks His Mercy. His Divine Mercy is for all as long as this world exists and while one is still alive, thereafter comes His judgement. Then it will be required from all how His commandment was kept. "If you did not eat my Flesh and drink my Blood you have no life in you, my Flesh is food indeed" It would be a great disappointment for one to hear on that day from Jesus "I do not know you" whereas one has the chance now to take His Words seriously.

The Apostles and the early Christians celebrated the Lord's Death and Resurrection as our Lord Jesus Christ instructed His Church, on green Thursday to be doing until He comes. "And they devoted themselves to the apostles' teaching and fellowship, to the breaking of bread and prayers" Acts 2 vs 42. This the Catholic Church has been faithfully doing as was handed to Her by the Apostles down the ages. Jesus is present in the Holy Eucharist, the Holy communion which we receive is Jesus, Body, Blood, Soul and Divinity just as St. Paul said "The bread which we break is it not the body of Jesus and the cup which we drink the blood of Jesus" Well, it is a free choice to accept or reject the truth but the Truth remains. Jesus is the Truth, He is God and His word remains forever. God does not change. No one can change Him. We either accept Him as He is or reject Him.

Nevertheless, the knocking sound inside the house stopped, but continued outside until our stay at home was over and we went back to the city. However, while still in the village, on New Year's Eve, the family prepared yam porridge with crayfish for lunch. An African dish I usually enjoyed eating, since my childhood, whenever it is well cooked. When lunch was served me, gladly I began eating it with appetite. But hardly did I finish chewing the first bite, swallowing became very difficult. My throat was completely blocked and I began vomiting blood, struggling for air. My mother, sister and other members of the family present were in panic not knowing how to help me. They offered me water, I could not drink it. I felt as though there was a long nail across my neck that almost got me choked. It was frightening. I thought that was the end. But in my relationship with Jesus that was not the way I expected to be called home. That was far from it. In my utter confusion and helplessness, therefore, I turned to our Blessed Mother and said three Hail Mary's.

Thereafter, I told Jesus if that was His Holy Will, then I accept it, if not He should remove it. In that very instant, that very second, it was removed. What a relief! That I did not die was God's Mercy. Who would want to harm someone who tried to do him good by sounding a tone of warning for him to take precaution not to land in hell, but the agent of evil spirits, Emeka, for such people do not appreciate good. That was his manner of showing gratitude for my indirect attempt to touch his conscience to save him from perdition. To confirm my suspicion, however, in the evening of the same day he telephoned my sister Ifeoma to wish her a happy new year. That was unusual. He was never in the habit of doing so. The ushering-in of the New Year usually begins at mid-night and not about five or six pm. He had hoped to be informed of the success of his wickedness but God is with me. "If God be for us who can be against us?"

The God I serve and worship is the Almighty Father, Creator of Heaven and Earth. The Eternal Father Who has all Powers. He is a protective and loving Father. He takes care of His Children who put their trust in Him. As God's child, I have forgiven Anthony and Emeka because God, my Father, asked me do so. All they have done to me and mine I have forgiven them but as Agents of evil spirits, God's enemy, I have nothing in common with them and never will. I hate the evil in them because God hates evil. Light and darkness have nothing in common. They chose willfully to serve God's enemy, enemy of my sweet Beloved Heavenly Father, therefore, that, I cannot forgive them. I cannot forgive their pretense to be angels of light, preaching about God, holding Church titles, living in deception, whereas they are agents of Satan. "Vengeance is mine I will repay says the Lord." The Lord fights the battle for His Children. As far as I am concerned, having realized, out of God's Mercy, Emeka is an agent of evil spirits, he is not the husband of my sister Eugenia for Light and darkness have nothing in common. God does not approve such a marriage.

A marriage contracted under camouflage and deceit is void. Nothing is hidden under the sun which would not be exposed in due time. Besides, the omniscient God cannot join such a marriage. My sister is a child of God, she loves Him and God in His infinite Mercy will grant her joy in Heaven as she has not known happiness in this world. The belief in God's Goodness and the trust in His Divine Mercy guarantees me the assurance of my sister's complete deliverance in due course. He will vindicate me and grant my sons Emmanuel and Peter the Grace to realize the need to separate themselves emotionally from Anthony and fill the vacuum in their heart with Jesus Who is their Father, embrace Mary their Mother and fight for their Father's Kingdom as Kings Children should. I am only their Care-taker for Jesus and Mary. They have no share in Anthony's wickedness, their destiny is Heaven because they belong to Jesus and Mary. They were given to me, in my misery, as children of consolation.

VIII. Falling in love

Unable to prevent the inevitable, I asked God, ignorantly, to take my mother's life and spare Anthony's. As already mentioned, it was instigated by the immense torture of his tongue for being the cause of his mother's death. The information he received from his prayer left me with no option but to wonder how that could be. However, in the course of time I came to know it was prompted by Satan to ease him of the guilt of his evil activities towards members of his own family, having sold his soul to the devil in pursuit of wealth which he never realized. He gambled and wasted his God-given life for perdition. Having been brainwashed to believe he prayed, while I was battling with my life at the hospital after the delivery of my son Peter, he chose my life to his mother's he said, which led to his mother's death. I was left with no other option than to do the same in order to balance the equation and relieve myself of the mental strain. However, my prayer which was said to the Almighty God my father taught me to pray to, was to my favor. My mother, then at the point of death, regained her health. For my benefit, Anthony's life was saved, for me to realize to whom he sold his soul, yet another opportunity for him to denounce Satan and chose Life, but he remained adamant.

The year 2006 was a turning point in my Christian life. It was the year I first observed the lenten period penitentially. I had never taken interest in observing the fasten period, whereas, fasting was not a strange word to me, as I grew up in a family where fasting was more or less a routine. All the ethics I observed in my parental home were all toppled by Anthony due to his "prayer." It was not necessary to fast as long as one kept awake until twelve mid-night, he told me. He called it "watching night" He compelled me not to sleep until eleven pm, as a treatment for my low blood pressure. Heaven help me if I dared! I was always told off, roughly treated and I felt lonely. How I missed the four walls of my parental home. How I missed my father! Unware he was an agent of evil spirits, it never occurred to me they usually had their meetings from twelve mid-night till four in the morning. Therefore, if I slept at eleven pm I would be fast asleep when he would leave his body for their meetings, giving them opportunity to do whatever they liked with me.

However, after his stroke he could no longer dictate to me when I should sleep and when not. I did not need permission from him any more to attend Mass or to pray. When God answered my prayer, saved my mother's life and his, I became aware I could pray direct to God and not only through him. It had not yet occurred to me then he was an agent of evil spirits, although I was beginning to realize his wickedness, wondering how God could bestow such a gift to such a one. Well, I always dismissed it knowing God's ways are not the ways of man.

Nevertheless, I fasted for the whole period of lent, from morning until 3 o'clock in the evening, using the prayer of St. Bridget of Sweden. A very powerful prayer which seemed to me as though it was written for me. I could not stop weeping for my sins and for all Jesus had to suffer for love of me. It was during this period I realized how much I hurt Jesus and how deep His Love for me is. I was so ashamed of myself for my ingratitude for all He suffered for me. His unjust trial, His silence, the awareness God Himself paid for my sins, seeking for my love, was indeed heart-rending. The thought Jesus died of a broken heart, after all the extreme torture, his agony and "what is there that Thou could have done for us which Thou hast not done!" was too much sorrow for my poor wretched heart.

Consequently, I saw myself, in a dream, on a road in construction, tractors blocking everywhere. The only possible passage was very narrow between very muddy dirty swamp, black and nauseating. In trying to pass through the narrow path, aiming at not falling into the swamp, hardly did I take a few step, I fell into the unavoidable dirty, black, smelling, formidable, and nauseating swamp. There was no one in sight. It was very eerie. The whole place was deserted. Suddenly, there was a man from nowhere who helped me out and led me to his nearby house where he had my clothes washed by himself. There was feasting and merriment in his house. The kindness and humility of the man instigated me to inform a girl I took for his daughter, her father was very humble and kind like my father. She simply answered "He is" I am most fortunate to be loved by such a Most Humble, Most Merciful and Good God.

Thereafter this prayer of St. Bridget became one of my favorite prayers which I say every year during lent. After the lent of 2007 I said this prayer every single day from 2007 until 2008 for my relations who are none Catholics for their salvation. I know that God is faithful to His words and I believe that God in His infinite Mercy will not forget any of them.

Just as He made my father accept His Church before calling Him Home He will also lead them to His Church on time.

This was how God cleansed me from my iniquity and restored life to my soul like the "prodigal son." My pastor also agreed with me my dream was God's Mercy revealed to me. As God would have it, a later confirmation of this Mercy was in another dream shown to me around October 2011. In this dream I dreamt of Saint Padre Pio preaching to a sea of people. My attempt to reach him was to no avail. However, somehow, I saw him alone and heard him tell me "your sins are forgiven" Oh, how I needed this confirmation. It was important for me due to my inability to make complete confession as a result of the kind of life I lived during the time of Anthony. I usually received the Holy Eucharist believing to be in a state of Grace, although I did not confess any old sins, taking it for granted they were forgiven, but having confessed to Anthony, an agent of Satan, when I thought he was acting for God, coupled with the sinful life with him, made me doubt sometimes. So this dream was a great relief for which I am very grateful to God.

Another extraordinary thing I experienced was equally in the year 2006 as I was coming out from the sacristy, after collecting the confirmation program for Grace. All of a sudden I saw the Holy Spirit leaving the Altar like a cloud, like incense, through the window. Actually, at the time I did not realize the Grace our Heavenly Father granted me. While He was still moving out the priest came into the Church from the sacristy. I asked him if he saw what I was seeing, he did not neither did the pianist. Somehow the priest dismissed it telling me it was smoke from the candle, but I knew what I saw because smoke from the candle could never be as much and bright moving out like incense. Anyway he later agreed with me it could not have been from the candle. I felt very sure of what I saw after seeing the display of cloud in EWTN during the chaplet of St. Michael. In fact I am very grateful for the work the Almighty Father used His daughter, Mother Angelica to achieve. EWTN is indeed an asset to the Church, a means to enrich Catholics in their faith, for the conversion of sinners and for the reunion of the Church, the Body of Christ. A means for the new evangelization before His second coming. EWTN portrays the Beauty and Magisterium of the Catholic Church.

Now at this point I was beginning to forge a relationship with Jesus. I became more aware of His presence in my life and the more I prayed the closer He drew near to me. One day, during the chaplet of St. Michael on EWTN the child Jesus, in the Arms of the Blessed Virgin, blessed me like in Benediction after Mass. It gave me such a thrill and excitement that made me telephone my brother in America, Lawrence, who was then living in New York to inform him. He shared my joy with me, showed surprise, although not Catholic, he was happy for me. This was the beginning of the beautiful experiences I had and still have with Jesus, of the awareness of my falling in love with my Savior.

In the scripture Jesus said where your treasure is there your heart is also. To my utter surprise and delight I found my thoughts always on Jesus. I began to discover I never did a thing without Him. I would include Him in my daily life. Everything I did Jesus was there and my heart began to glow with joy. Before I knew it my life became a prayer. I began to live a prayer life, a Eucharistic life. I could not live any more without Jesus. Mass became a daily objective. Sometimes I would attend Mass three times a day. My whole life changed completely. I realized the things that interested me before no longer do. Fear of death and Satan became strange words to me. My life began to have a meaning and I experienced peace and tranquility within my soul. I began to love what Jesus loves and hate all that He hates. I love Him body and soul. I gave Him my all, total surrender like a baby in its mother's arms. My heart belongs to Jesus. It is no longer I that live, but Jesus who dwells in me, just like my brother Saint Paul.

On one occasion, in my dream, Jesus addressed me with my maiden name, informed me He may marry me. When I woke up I took Him to His words for I did believe the dream. Although I did not know how that was to take place I was thrilled with the thought of being His Bride. As time went by I did not give thought to this dream any more until that blessed December 2010 when I received from the court the divorce documents. The authority that set me free to fly to the skies with happiness for being rid of a marriage that never was. It was then I remembered Jesus addressed me, in my dream, with my maiden name and confirmed my notion that no marriage ever existed between me and Anthony.

Anthony was a man who always said what he did not mean. He would always murmur something to himself, inaudible to the listener perhaps that was exactly what he did with the fake vow he made, saying one thing and murmuring another to himself, besides, light and darkness has nothing in common. He knew there was no marriage existing between us and always made it clear to me with his constant reminder I was not his wife. He would not hesitate to inform me he was already married to a girl in his village chosen for him by his mother.

However, despite his constant reminder I was not his wife, I consoled myself with the belief he made a vow before God, otherwise, I would not be living with him. At the time, I knew nothing of his dark side yet I wondered why he always refuted vehemently we were not married and accused me of putting the wedding ring on his wrong finger which made everything void. Nevertheless, I am most fortunate he made no vow having murmured something else within himself. Had I the slightest hint it would have been the key to an early escape from that pit of hell. So one can just imagine how happy I was when all the hanky panky was over. Having recalled to mind the promise Jesus made to me in the dream, that He may marry me, I pawned the wedding ring of Anthony immediately on the third January 2011 after I miraculously found it where I dumped it, together with some coins for donations at Mass, and forgot it.

Prior to the day that ring was found, I had already made a thorough search in vain. The money got from the pawn was donated to the poor. Thereafter, I had all the wedding pictures torn, got myself cut out from one of them and put it on the Divine Mercy picture of Jesus hanging on the wall in my bedroom. The next thing was to destroy all the pictures in the album, family video films, hence he was not family, besides, for me is Jesus the Father of my sons and Mary their Mother. I am simply their care-taker. The remaining pictures were very few, those without him that left no trace of him on the background. It did not matter if the pictures spoke of the childhood of my children, all were destroyed, for good.

Thereafter, with the destruction of his pictures, my next step was to remove every possible trace of him. The furniture was thrown away and replaced with new ones. The apartment renovated and painted.

Now, due to the Mercy of God I can breathe again. I was now ready to begin life afresh. For this reason I went to the confessional. The life with Anthony and the diplomat who fathered Antonia I regarded as sinful, therefore, I confessed them as such. One can understand the reason for the joy in my heart when Saint Padre Pio confirmed my sins are forgiven.

A series of beautiful dreams about Saints such as Saint Thomas the Apostle, Saint John Paul II and dreams about the resurrection of Jesus Christ followed. It was granted me, in the dream, to know my daughter-in-law, Tamara was to have two children, having waited long for the fruit of the womb. I informed them they would have a boy and a girl. Today, they have a son and a daughter, Junior and Angelina, according to my dream. Honestly, I cannot thank God enough for all the benefits, considering my unworthiness, a nonentity that I am, less than half of an ant. However, it is interesting to know that the holy people of God do not forget, in Heaven, the souls they consider their charge while on earth. As Saint John Paul II was Pope, I informed him of my dilemma with Anthony, although then I did not realize the person I was living with was an agent of the devil. I wrote to inform him of the unceasing quarrel, thinking I was the cause of it all, to which he replied he prayed for me. He did not forget me. Our good God blessed me with a dream about him in Heaven. When I saw him he was beaming with life and vitality, young, and in his early thirties, very happy. There was a sea of people getting ready for Mass but as I was about to go he gave me a little girl. When I woke up joy filled my heart. I informed my son and his wife they would have another child and this time a baby girl. Shortly after that Angelina was born. Junior and Angelina are consecrated to the Sacred Heart of Jesus and to the Immaculate Heart of Mary.

In fact I am most unworthy, but God is merciful unto me a miserable sinner. Our Lord Jesus Christ is all He said He is. To please Him He has to be trusted. Out of His Goodness, Saint John Paul II appeared to me again in the dream, standing before a sea of people, this time he was being cheered and the people were rejoicing because of him. However, I did not realize the meaning of the dream until his beatification was announced. Oh, how happy I felt he shared this experience with me. He is my brother and intercessor. Although I love every Pope, he is my favorite.

Sometimes, on a cross road, in utter despair, a cry of the heart reaching out to God in confidence is usually not in vain. I can still remember in 1975, after I was caged in by Anthony, and I saw there was no way out for me any more for the die was cast, I found myself into what I never bargained for. One day, looking out of the window, my eyes focused towards Heaven, totally depressed and confused, I asked God for Mercy. I asked Him to at least grant me happiness in Heaven. It was a cry from the heart for I saw no chance of happiness in this world. I had no idea this cry was heard, although it took thirty-three years to realize it, yet it is worth it. The Joy in my heart today has removed every trace of the ugly experience. No troubled water can persist in the midst of God's love.

When I began falling in love with Jesus I cannot say, it simply happened. God's love is too good to be true and yet, it is true, I am in love with God, with Jesus. I believe, with constant prayer I gradually fell in love before I knew it. I cannot move hand or foot without asking him. He makes decisions for me as He is the center of my life. That I have no more fear is because Jesus is always by me. Sometimes, I hear Him talking to me and sometimes we chat as though He was standing before me. Sometimes, the conversation moves me to smile or laugh. Sometimes, I would think I was just imagining things but I was not. I do sometimes chat with Jesus. One needs to develop a personal relationship with Him. It is amazing. I never thought this heart of mine will ever know love. I used to wonder, when I used to watch films, having had no love-life until now, I wondered how people could shout with joy "I'm in love". I developed interest in watching romantic movies and series like "The bold and the beautiful" as there was no love in my life in order to make up for it by watching others who were in love, even though it was fiction. It was a kind of addiction watching such series, films, reading romantic novels in an attempt to fill the vacuum in my heart, to alleviate my misery.

Thanks to our Lord Jesus Christ I do not have need for such any more. Now, I have a much better experience with true love in the real sense of it. Oh, it's so beautiful being loved by God. I love Him because He first loved me. How patiently my Beloved was waiting for me while I was in the wilderness of sin. How I must have hurt Him! How He must love me! Now I am in His Arms, nothing can ever change that, not any more, He will not allow it. I'm in good Hands now and forever. He has always loved me, but I never realized it, oh it hurts to think of it. I feel so unworthy, most wretched, a nobody, less than half of an Ant, a Cinderella, to be loved by the Almighty God. But His Love grants me the courage to love Him. O, how He won my admiration, stooping so low for me to reach Him. What a humble God we have! I am so fortunate for the love and affection Jesus showers on me unworthy though I am. Now I am loved and I love. My sweet Jesus has found me and I am at home in His Arms. I thank God from the very depth of my heart. I do not deserve, but I am happy and grateful to be loved. I thank Jesus for teaching me what Love is. How good it is to be taught by the Beloved. What a tender loving teacher. I became a young girl again. I feel like a teenager in love. The Lord restored what the cankers have eaten. I feel very secure in His Most Sacred Heart. I love Him in the Eucharist.

Before Antonia went to the hostel I drove with her one day, while waiting for the traffic light to turn green, all of a sudden, water was poured on the windscreen of the car, on the driver's side. Antonia was sitting in front beside me, but the water, although it was like a bucket full, did not reach her, only on my side. It was not raining and there was neither trees nor houses close by from where one could assume it came. The water was from Heaven. Water, a symbol of baptism, was poured on me.

God used it for my cleansing and restoration to the stage I was before I diverged from Christian norms into sin. God alone can put back the clock. Therefore, now that Jesus put back the clock, I was free for Him to make me His bride, as He mentioned in my dream when He called me with my maiden name and said He may marry me. I desired to be a nun, as it had been my childhood desire to serve Him before straying away like the prodigal son. Not being then a Catholic contributed a great deal to my fall. However, I do not live in a monastery. My four walls is my monastery, Jesus is my Spiritual director as there is scarcity of priests. Mary, my sweet loving Mum is my guide. Although it is preferable to live in a monastery, to belong to a community therefore, whoever has the opportunity should seize it. Besides, it is indeed good to serve the Lord in a consecrated life, especially when one is young.

However, this was the state of event in my life, an empty life, having nothing to look forward to or hope for until Jesus entered into it, filled it and made it worth living. He washed my past away out of His Mercy, made me His Bride, bestowed me with Graces for which I am most unworthy. Sometimes, the thought of His infinite Love for me overwhelms me. He forgave me my sins, restored my life, gave me His Love and fills me with Graces. I must say, the tranquility in my heart is too good to be true and yet it is true. Eternity would be too short to express the gratitude in my Heart for the Love of God. Now I have a love story. I have a right to love as everyone has a right to. My Love is my God.

IX. Being in love

How can I describe this love that fills my heart,
This beautiful intoxicating love between my poor
little heart and the Most Sacred Heart of my Creator,
My Sweet Beloved, my only Love, the Love of my life.

Oh! so sweet it be, as sweet as sweet can be, sweeter
than honey, more intoxicating than wine, pure, sweet,
Divine. Oh, my sweet Love, sweet Treasure of my heart,
my heart sings to You, uncomposed songs of sweet
melodies of love, in this little heart of mine, so poor.

Oh, so little for all the love, over-flowing, for my sweet
Treasure, Jesus. Yet, these uncomposed, sweet melodies
of love reach the Most Sacred Heart of my sweet Love.
There they are tenderly treasured, cherished for all eternity.

Oh, poor heart mine, so enriched with Love Divine, my sweet
Creator, a teenager's heart thee doth make, for love so utterly
beautifully Divine, the Most Sacred Heart of my Beloved, to
cherish, adore and love so dearly. Oh, how sweet is the Love
of my life, Jesus, Beloved of my heart, my eternal Happiness.

Oh, poor wretched heart mine, though wretched thou no
longer be, enriched thou be with Divine Presence of Love
so Divine. Though a teenager's heart thou be, yet infatuation
knoweth thou not. True Love, sacrificial Love, beautiful, and
soothing, taught by Beloved so sweet, thou doth knoweth.

Oh, what a sweet Darling, my sweet Love, sweet Redeemer,
my Jesus is. Oh, my sweet Creator, how I love Thee! oh, How

beautiful, how pure Love Divine is! How sweet it is to be loved by Jesus, my sweet Love. At last, a love story do I have. In love with my God. Yes, the love of my life, my darling Sweet Creator is.

At last in June 2010 Jesus made me His bride on the feast of the Sacred Heart. On this day, the CFC, couples for Christ to which I belonged, had a general assembly, but I left the meeting to attend the Mass which was more important to me. I love the Eucharist, therefore, I always made sure I was in a state of Grace. I received every month or every forth-night the sacrament of reconciliation. It did not matter if I was aware of venial sin or not. On this particular evening I experienced the beauty of God's love for the first time. Actually, at first, I did not realize what was happening to me, the Grace granted me, and began praying against it until I remembered Saint Magaret Mary Alacoque and Saint Faustina. Saint Faustina, in her diary, said Jesus grants such favor to very few people, therefore, I realized the great favor Jesus granted me, a nonentity and a wretched creature, so unworthy. I was so grateful to be loved by God.

I believe my relationship with Jesus began to grow after the Benediction of the child Jesus in the Arms of the blessed Virgin during the chaplet of St. Michael in EWTN with mother Angelica. I immediately fell in love with the child Jesus and always addressed Him ever since, lovingly, as my sweet little brother Jesus. I have been favored with several dreams of Jesus where I spent time with Him. On one occasion, I think it was on the sixteenth of October 2011, Jesus allowed me a sweet dream in which He gave me, with His facial gesture, the feeling we both have something in confidence, just for Him and me. He did not desire others around to know. I woke up remembering I had a baby boy in my arms and was filled with joy. My heart accepted it as a sign of an answered prayer having asked Jesus to grant my son and his wife another child who would care for them because Junior and Angelina have been consecrated to His Most Sacred Heart and to the Immaculate Heart of Mary. I can still see the

Face of Jesus in that dream and His facial gesture still thrills me. I am a most fortunate little nothing to be granted God's Love in such a measure.

On 20.10.2011, just before I went to bed I had such a strong desire for Jesus. When there was no sign of Him I felt He did not care, but of course He does. In my dream I spent time with Him. First He appeared in a large screen Television in which I was privileged, alone, to see Him. Everyone I asked could not see Him. On the Screen Hitler and the Nazi soldiers were parading. In short I saw the horrible war of the atheistic regime. In the same dream, but in another place, two children, brothers, fell into a pit. Nobody could save them, but having seen Jesus was around I drew courage from His Presence, jumped into the very pit, saved the two brothers and gave them to their ungrateful parents. Still in the same dream I saw a group of three men, one of them put his hand on me, but I resented it and warned him "my body is holy" consequently he removed his hand, apologetically. Somehow, I noticed Jesus was pleased. He drew nearer to watch my reaction towards the man. On seeing my resentment towards the man, He went back to His seat. Again in the same dream as I was about to lift up a heavy object Jesus came forward to assist me making sure it was not heavy for me. It was a great joy when I wake up from this dream. My happiness knew no bound.

I realized Jesus cares very much about me. His jealousy spoke it all. However, the dream about Hitler and the Nazis, the atheistic regime, was for me to see how Satan mobilized God's children and still mobilizes them to offend God. Children for whom Jesus shed His Most Precious Blood, a bitter price for their salvation fail to realize how much He loves them. They keep hurting Him unnecessarily. The ingratitude of the parents of the children saved from the pit, shows the Graces God grants me are for saving souls, to God's Glory, even if they are ungrateful. I am only the instrument of God. It is no longer I that live, but Jesus who dwells in me. When my time comes Jesus and Mary will come for me, by the Grace of God. I am in the world, but I'm not of the world. My Home is Heaven by Jesus and Mary.

On Tuesday 25.10.2011, I was in Heaven on earth. My soul was completely united with the Soul of Jesus. This day our souls became completely kneaded together like in a dough. I gave Him my heart completely and from this day onwards my soul became free to soar above the earth into Heaven enveloped in the ecstasy of His Divine Love. I often tell Jesus I am so unworthy for all the Graces and Favors He grants me. God is unfathomably Merciful. His Love is for everyone, old and young. Everyone is a child before Him. He is not partial. We are all His unworthy children. How fortunate we are to be created and loved by God. Unworthy though we are, He showers us with Graces and Favors.

Oh, if we Catholics would realize what we have, the richness of our Catholic Faith, we would all be Saints. It is not suffice to be Catholic and not practice the Faith. The trouble with us is that most of us are underlings, cowards and insincere. Remember, Jesus said He stands at the door and knocks, He enters into the hearts of those who receive Him. Mum, the blessed Virgin, told Saint Faustina the Graces are for everyone. Think of it this way, one receives as he gives and as he trusts. On this very day, after glancing through the diary of Saint Faustina, I became very much down feeling I was not reaching Jesus, at the same time wishing I would have liked to have done something great for Him. But Jesus thought me, like Saint Therese, the little flower, it did not matter how little we could do as long as we did it with our whole heart, for love of Him. We all have special assignments for Him. I felt I am an ungrateful daughter. I failed to see all the Goodness of God towards me. I regretted badly and asked for God's pardon and He forgave me.

One must not live in a monastery or in a convent to live a religious or consecrated life, though it is preferable. Our four walls can be our convent. It all depends on how much we love Jesus. Everyone is not fortunate to discover his or her vocation in a consecrated life, all is not favored to grow up in Catholic homes. As in my case, being raised up in a good Christian home where family prayers were conducted three times a day, 6 am, 12 noon and about six, six-thirty in the evening, a regular attendance of daily church services, I would have ended up a nun in a convent at an early age. But unfortunately there was no motivation for religious or consecrated life, no encouragement for a Saintly life. Thus it was impossible for one to realize one's vocation, in that respect, a great disadvantage of not being catholic.

The Catholic Church makes Saints. Nevertheless, God in His infinite Mercy knows His children, those the Father has given Him, where-ever they are He will find them and bring them back to the flock as His desire is for all to be under one flock. For this reason He granted my father, His humble servant, like the thieve who became a saint on the cross, the Grace to be Catholic before He called him Home. God is always faithful, patiently and eagerly waiting to draw anyone who makes even the slightest effort to reach Him, to Himself.

Once again I must mention the most bitter experience I had at the knowledge of the agony in the Most Sacred Heart of Jesus, the day I had the opportunity to watch His revelation to Saint Margaret Mary Alacoque about His Sacred Heart on EWTN. His statement "Will no one have pity on this Heart?" the fact He would not mind going through the same ordeal again if only His Love was reciprocated, touched me greatly reducing me to tears. The Almighty God, Creator of Heaven and earth, Author and Giver of Life asking me to have pity on Him. That was too much for me and I wept bitterly. I began to see God with a different view. He became more admirable in my sight than I ever thought possible. I should be the one to ask Him to have pity on me and there He is asking me to have pity for Him. What a merciful and humble God! I began to see God's true nature and to understand why He forfeited so much and suffered so much for me and you. If God could be so humble and suffered so much for me what stops me from being like Him.

Thereafter, on 30.11.2010 I surrendered everything to Jesus and consecrated myself to His Most Sacred Heart in the very words of Saint Margret Mary Alacoque:

Sacred Heart of my Lord and Savior Jesus Christ, to Thee I consecrate and offer up my person and my life, my actions, trials and sufferings that my entire being may henceforth only be employed in loving, honoring and glorifying Thee. This is my irrevocable will, to belong entirely to Thee, and to do all for thy love renouncing with my whole heart all that can displease Thee. I take Thee, O Sacred Heart, for the sole object of my love, the protection of my life, the pledge of my salvation. The remedy of my frailty and inconstancy, the reparation for all the defects of my life and my secure Refuge at the hour of death. Be Thou O most merciful Heart, my justification before God Thy Father, and screen me from His anger which I have so justly merited. I fear all from my own weakness and malice, and placing my entire confidence in Thee, O Heart of love, I hope all from Thine infinite goodness, annihilate in me all that can displease Thee or resist Thee. Imprint Thy pure love so deeply in my heart that I may never forget thee or be separated from Thee. I beseech Thee through thine infinite goodness grant that my name be engraved on Thee for in this I place all my happiness and all my glory to live and die as one of Thy devoted servants – Amen!

Gradually, as time went by, I realized God created us in a unique way, no two people can identify themselves as the same. Each individual is unique, one cannot be the other. God relates to every individual in a unique way. In order to enhance my relationship with God I had to reconsecrate myself to Him in my own words. I must mean every word in my consecration. Therefore, on 26.02.2011, about three months after the consecration in the words of Margret Mary Alacoque I reconsecrated myself to the Most Sacred Heart of Jesus in my own words as follows:

Strayed away in the wilderness, your love sustained me O my Beloved. Through the window strayed my eyes searching for You O sweet Love of my heart crying out to you in distress, pleading for happiness in your Eternal Kingdom, as my heart sought helplessly, in utter loneliness, for love and recognition in this life and found none. But You were there with outstretched Arms beckoning me with eyes full of love and desire for my love. Through all the thorns and pains of slight, maltreatment, disregard and contempt, prompted by the ignorant link to evil, through his agent, you watched over me day and night. You shielded me from their darts with your Precious Blood. At the fullness of time You rescued me and You put back the clock, which only You can do, Oh, sweet love of my heart. I hereby, in the Presence of the Almighty Father, the Blessed Virgin Mary, my Mum, all the Saints and Angels, consecrate myself, all that I am, body and soul, to You Most Sacred Heart of my Beloved. To You I give my Freewill, which is the only thing I possess that is mine, as a sign of my loyalty, faithfulness and fidelity, O Sacred Heart of my Beloved. My sweet Love, I seek nothing of my own, but to be Your Bride, to abide always in Your Love and Grace and to remain in Your Arms until I come to You in Heaven to worship, adore, praise and love You throughout Eternity with Your Saints and Angels. I desire to be there where You are. Mold me as You want me to be dearest Jesus and permit me to share with You Your Joys and Sorrows. I desire to identify myself with Your suffering, but be always by me like a mother and suffering would be sweet suffering in love – Amen!

I have been experiencing Jesus in a special way, I do not know yet His Holy Will for me, but He will make it known. At moment I am only swimming in His love and fear has become a strange word to me. The fear of death and the care about my burial was a hangover I could not get rid of, but now Jesus has taken care of that worry off me. He takes care of me and mine and of all my affairs. I have surrendered myself completely to Him like a baby in it's mother's arms.

Frankly speaking, it is a great feeling being loved by God and loving Him. In every Catholic Church Jesus is present in the Tabernacle, just as He said He will be with us till the end of time. Moreover, it is better to believe without seeing, an act of Faith is required. He is really there and it is a great privilege to have His Divine Presence with us. Think of God humbling Himself, because He loves, to be with us, in the Host, imprisoned in our Tabernacles. We seek God, but He lives in our Tabernacles day and night waiting to be visited. Did He not say to Nicodemus, "What is Spirit is Spirit", a doubtful mind cannot experience Him and to experience Him requires patience and in His Terms. It is Jesus, Body, Blood, Soul and Divinity we receive in the Host in Holy Communion. Jesus is the Eucharist. I receive Him, experience Him and I love receiving Him. I love the Eucharist. I cannot live without Him therefore, I live a Eucharistic life.

On 30.10.2011, forgetting the time was set back for winter, I found myself an hour earlier in the church. Somehow, I felt Jesus wanted me earlier to spend time with Him in the Tabernacle. I always like to spend time with Him in the Tabernacle before the Mass starts, even if it was only about five or ten minutes depending on the time of my arrival.

This particular day the Lord somehow needed my company and I experienced Him in a very special way. Jesus is my best friend, He knows everything about me, I have no secret before Him. He is the best friend one can ever have. If one is open, and sincere with Him, trusting Him entirely, having delight in doing His Will and being oneself, that is all it takes to have a wealth of peace, joy and equilibrium. Ever since my relationship with Jesus I have everything. Jesus is very affectionate, He cares a lot about the comfort of His beloved. I once felt chilly, and I did the very natural thing a heart in love would do. Spontaneously, glancing at the Sacred Heart picture, I uttered, as I sneaked under the eiderdown" Sweetheart, it is very cold", before I knew it I felt a stream of warmth run into my body warming me up. I felt like a child being protected from cold by his mother. What a wonderful experience. There is nothing Jesus will not do for His friends and there is nothing I will not do for Him, by His Grace. I share with Him His Joys and His sorrows.

I can well remember the day I brought home the Sacred Heart framed photograph which I have in my bedroom. The joy in my heart that very day I cannot describe it. It was as though my sweet Beloved has been away for a very long period of time and was returning to our newly renovated, furnished home. I was taking my sweet Beloved home, and as I drove the car with care not to damage the glass I spoke as though He was physically there with me. I loved talking with Him. On reaching Home I hung the picture where I thought suitable for it, but shortly after I heard a loud crash, behold it was my most precious picture, but to my utter surprise the picture did not break, except for a slight piece on the right corner, probably to remind me I once placed it at the wrong place. The picture was completely undamaged. Joyfully, thanking God, I hung the picture once again back on the same place making sure the nail was strong enough to hold it.

After hanging it I asked God not to allow it to fall again. Few hours later, the picture fell again with a loud crash that almost frightened me out of my life. How would I get the money to replace such an expensive picture I thought. To my utter surprise nothing happened to the picture. How could it fall from such a height, hitting the writing table before falling to the floor without breaking, for a second time. I was somewhat scared wondering if Jesus did not want His picture to be in the room. Suddenly, it seemed I was made to notice a hook on a more lower place where I can always see Him whenever I enter the room and you know what, the picture has been hanging there all the time.

This made me realize how much Jesus desires me to always take notice of Him and why not, He is my first love, my only love, the love of my life and I cannot live without Him. Had it not been for Jesus I would never have thought of hanging the picture there. Actually, Jesus Himself arranged our apartment. The furniture are His choice and the pictures hang where He wants them to be. I live with Him and Mum, His Holy Angels watch over us while my sisters and brothers – the Saints – watch over me and pray for me to the Lord our God. All the pictures hang where He desires them to hang. I have never been in love before, but now I am. Is that not great? That Jesus, my sweet wonderful Savior is my LOVE! He taught me what love is, gave me His love, I reciprocated with all my heart and having a wonderful time. Well, suffering can be painful, but what is love without suffering. To share joy and suffering with the Beloved is love, suffer together and enjoy together.

11.12.2010, as I knelt down absorbed in prayer at home, in my private altar, expressing to God my desire to share with Him His suffering, His joys and sorrow, suddenly as I prayed, I cannot explain how the hands I folded in prayer were spread open, a sudden movement transpired on my palms as though something was sprayed into my palms, before I knew it, my sweet Beloved, Jesus, granted me the Grace to bear His stigmata. Being a considerate, compassionate, loving God, He granted me a hidden stigmata, the marks of his five wounds. Perhaps, for the fact I am not living in a monastery, where such marks would be much better understood and appreciated than otherwise. Not that it would have bothered me though, all that matters to me is what my Beloved thinks of me, nothing more and nothing less, as long as I please Him. Jesus always has His own reasons for whatever He does. Our part is to show appreciation. God knows us better than we know ourselves. Every action of His is prompted by love. The Stigmata pains respectively, sweet pains of love, and from them come sweet smelling perfumes. I am such a nonentity, very unworthy and wretched. In fact less than half of an Ant, and yet the Lord grants me such a favor and showers me with such love and affection. I remember telling Jesus sometime I want to suffer with Him and I heard Him say, in my heart, "you are suffering with me". Then I did not understand what He meant, but as time went on I did. It is of great joy, a privilege for me to suffer with

Jesus. Suffering with Him is not a burden for me, He always grants the Grace to bear. Love is everything. Jesus is always ready and willing to bear every suffering with us provided we invite Him to do so.

My Altar, a prayer corner in my living-room, consecrated by my parish priest, is decorated with the picture of the Divine Mercy, a crucifix of the precious Blood, the picture of the crown of Thorns, a framed picture of our Lady of all nations, a framed picture of our Lady of perpetual succour. In the center, a large tapestry picture of the Sacred Heart, the tapestry is for me my Monstrance and the face of Jesus the consecrated Host made visible. His Face is always alive when I talk with Him in prayer. Sometimes, He gives me some flying kisses or a drop of His Tear in my eyes that rolls down my cheeks. I take it with my finger and kiss it. His tears are for me His kisses. I am not favored with the opportunity to adore my love as I would want to in our parish, unless I drive to the Cathedral which is about forty-five minutes' drive or I travelled to other countries on vacation, so He provided me with an alternative. There is no adoration in our parish, which is very sad indeed. Having made fruitless attempts to persuade my parish priest into creating room for adoration, at least once a month, I gave up when he told me the members of the committee were to decide, besides a tree cannot make a forest. It is not my place to advice the priests, but I presume the Lord would be pleased if we paid more attention to Him and grant Him the adoration which is to our own advantage.

May the Most Sacred Heart of Jesus, in the Blessed Sacrament, be praised, adored and loved with grateful affection, at every moment, in all the Tabernacles of the world, even until the end of time – Amen.

After I became very much acquainted with the Sacred Heart tapestry picture in my Altar, the looks in His eyes drives my heart crazy with love. This is because the picture becomes alive whenever I am in prayer standing before Him. He listens to me attentively with interest. His facial expressions enable me sense when He is delighted with whatever I discuss with Him and when He is not. In fact I feel His Divine Presence, as though He is physically present. Sometimes I feel His Divine Presence in me when He unites Himself with me. An act of Grace which I do not deserve, yet exceptionally grateful to God for uniting Himself to someone like me, a nobody, who is less than half of an ant. Words are not enough to express the delight in my heart. I feel very connected to Him. I have never been understood, before now, in my life. Jesus understands me. He grants me the Grace to be myself before Him. He is a great Lover.

Whoever reciprocates His love begins his Heaven here on earth as I am doing, everyone in a unique way. Jesus is there for everyone who hears His knocking, opens the door of the heart and lets Him in. Of course He is good to everyone even to those against him, after all, we are asked to love our neighbor as ourselves, to do good to those who hate us and despitefully use us, how much more God Who is Love and Merciful. But the problem begins after one expires to meet Him face to face on His judgement seat to give account of how one spent his life here on earth. It would be terrible for those who fail to keep His commandment "abide in My Love." My sympathy goes to those outside the One, Holy, Catholic and Apostolic Church which He founded. Any church without the Pope is not with Jesus. They do not possess the whole Truth. The Sacraments are incomplete.

If one does not know someone how can one establish a relationship with him. A relationship with Jesus is only possible if He is received in the Holy Eucharist. It is interesting to note the Orthodox Churches are on their way to reconciliation with the Pope. That is the right thing to do for humility is a virtue much appreciated by God. It is not right that brothers should not eat on the same Table, breaking the same Bread as did our brothers, the early Christians in Jerusalem under Peter. Our good Lord desires His Church to be united, to be under one Flock. For this reason He chose Peter to be His Vicar and maintain unity among

His brothers. Therefore, it is wise for the Patriarch of the Orthodox Churches to submit Himself under the Pope because it is the Holy Will of God. If we love Him we should swallow our pride and keep His commandments. After all, what are we struggling for if not to make Heaven, to share with Jesus His Divine Life. Then why should we not be one in Him as He is one with the Father? Why not accept His Vicar the Pope? Why do we try to change God? Let us not keep Jesus weeping, our Blessed Mother worried and shedding tears, rather let us be united and put the enemy of our Beloved Father, our enemy, Satan to shame.

I cannot wait for the time when I will be forever united with Jesus eternally in Heaven, to adore, worship, and praise Him with all His Holy Angels and Saints throughout Eternity, and be magnetized by His Beauty, drunk in His Love. For this end is no amount of suffering too much. Oh, how I thank Jesus for the Grace to swim in His Love here on earth.

> O Love Divine, Sweet Drink and Food of my soul,
> Life and Beauty of my soul, my Eternal Desire,
> King of my heart, Lord of my soul, my Most priceless
> Treasure, Most Beloved of my Heart, my Eternal
> Happiness, my Heaven, my Hope, the Melody in
> my heart, my Sweet All and All how I long for Thee.

Jesus asked Saint Margret Mary Alacoque to observe Gethsemane Hour, spontaneously I decided to do the same. At eleven pm on a Thursday I prostrated before the tapestry Sacred Heart picture in my altar without knowing how to observe the Hour. One Sunday, however, as I was coming home from Mass, pondering in my heart if I should forget about the Gethsemane hour, as the revelation was not for me, because I did not know how to observe it, I heard Jesus tell me "just be there for me" Therefore, I decided to continue, still not knowing how to observe it. Then one day my eyes glanced at the Precious Blood booklet my cousin sent me, containing the Revelations of Jesus to a certain Nigerian boy,

Barnabas, in a prayer group, which I simply dumped on my table in the living room, not fascinated with the portrait of Jesus as a black man. Instinctively I glanced through the pages and came across the Gethsemane Hour. At once I realized why Jesus asked me to just be there for Him. The Thursday night I observed the Gethsemane Hour with this booklet was the night I felt my name written in the Lambs book of Life. My relationship with Jesus deepened. I came closer to Him. Miracles do happen and Jesus is very generous in the distribution of His Graces.

That night, after the Gethsemane Hour, I went to bed, covered myself with the eiderdown, then, suddenly, just like the stigmata, as already mentioned, I did not know how the instinct to open my palms came, I did not know how I lay face upwards looking towards the ceiling. At once I heard the ringing of a bell, like in the liturgy of the Eucharist, during the consecration. An Angel of God, suddenly dropped water into my eyes. Ever since then I began to weep with Jesus. Whenever I am emotionally moved His tears drop from my eyes and rolls down my cheeks. What a blessing! The taste of the human tears is very salty, but His is almost without taste. I love receiving them regarding them as pearls and loving kisses from my one and only Love. The kisses of Him who has always loved me ever before He conceived the idea of creating me. Everything that proceeds from Him is fully and completely embedded in love. What a blessing to share emotions with my Love, God of Creation Who was, Who is and Who will ever be. The Devotion to His Most Precious Blood, as was revealed to Barnabas, is very essential. The Chaplet of the Precious Blood, on 12 red Beads for each Mystery. It is a very important Devotion for our time to be said immediately after the Holy Rosary of our Lady.

It is a privilege to share with Jesus His sufferings, His sorrows and His pains. I am very grateful to Him for the Grace to do so, for what would love be if lovers do not share everything together. I love what Jesus loves and hate what He hates. My will has been joined to His. I no longer have a will of my own. His Will is my will. Just as Jesus gave back everything

He received from the Father to the Father to become one with Him, I have given back to Him everything I received from Him to be one with Him. He has transformed me into Himself. He possesses me. I do not live for myself any longer. I live for Jesus. He takes care of everything for me, things I am unable to take care of He sees to them. He takes care of every single thing, no matter how minute. Things that need to be seen to in a household, Jesus my sweet Bridegroom sees to them. It is amazing. When it was difficult for me to screw the nail that held the venetian blind, on my bedroom window, off, it was bad and needed to be replaced, after I made several attempts in vain, I asked Jesus to help me, He is the only one I have, if He did not help me, no one else would. Immediately the nail became lose.

My tape-recorder with CD player which I play every night to listen to Christian songs before sleeping became defect. It may sound strange, but it is true, for Jesus nothing is strange when His Love is reciprocated. He gives His all. The CD player no longer indicated the number of songs on display and it stopped rotating. In short it stopped playing. I asked Jesus for help and it began to play. This is just to mention but a few. He knows those that are His for He searches the Heart. To reach Him one must be oneself in order to be able to be honest with Him. He does not accept lip service, no pretense. Humility is a virtue He mostly appreciates for He Himself is Humility. Jesus loves openness and Truth. Always say what you mean and not vain promises. This enables one enjoy His love and care. Do not expect things your own way. Should that be the case then you have not really understood Him. You must join your will to His Will. Pray for the Grace to do so. Be patient. Rom was not built in a day. A patient dog eats the fattest bone.

During Mass, on the feast of the Immaculate Conception, on 8.12.2011 the Lord, in His infinite Goodness, granted me a most loving Grace, the experience of the crowning with thorns. It lasted all through the Mass. Had I not been in love with Jesus, if I did not have the Grace to bear, I would not have been able to bear it without screaming for pain. Nobody noticed I was suffering in pain. Well Jesus never gives us what we cannot bear. This experience increased in me the sympathy for Jesus. It made me realize we do not comprehend what He had to bear for love of us. If we did He would not be in agony today. However, whatever pain I must have felt, it was simply nothing to what our good Lord had to bear with the crown of thorns that pierced Him, continuously, through His delicate Skin. How He must have suffered! I am beginning to understand the Saints. One begins to love suffering for the love of Jesus. My first experience of the crown of thorns was on 20.05.13, but not in such extent. These days I experience it regularly, in a lesser degree, almost at every Mass and sometimes at home. I do not deserve all the love and affection my sweet Jesus showers on me, His unworthy and wretched creature, a nobody, less than half of an Ant. I am but a nonentity, His love for me is overwhelming. I am very grateful to Jesus for this wonderful Grace to love Him. I am head over heels in love with Him. I love everything about Him, all He revealed Himself, through His Saints and through His Holy Church.

Once again, on the Sunday before the Pentecost, my Beloved granted me, the Grace to feel the crown of thorns in a greater degree. It lasted also throughout the Mass. Each time I experience the crown of thorns I cannot help but be engulfed in the thought of what Jesus went through. I remember His bitter passion, all the pain He endured. How He suffered different types of pain, all at once, from the hands of sadists. Remembering He is the Almighty God, by whom all things were created, Lord of Heaven and Earth, to be so inhumanly treated by His creatures. What He grants us to share with Him is actually nothing, no matter how painful it might seem to us. Moreover He grants us also the Grace to endure while He Himself suffered alone and died of a broken heart. Nevertheless, the pain I experienced did not rest only on the fore-head, it penetrated to the nerves of the nose and eyes. I cannot describe it, one has to experience it to understand. It was really piercing pain, yet what He made me feel was just too minute to what He experienced on His Sacred Head, the seat of

Wisdom. Each time I fell real sympathy for Him. How sad He gives so much and gets so little in return. Despite emptying Himself for love of us most of us deny Him love. Unrequited love is the most heart-rending experience. It must never escape the mind He is a Father, a protective and loving Father, the best Father, yearning for the love of His children.

> O, most Beloved mine, how I crave for Your Love.
> My heart yearns to identify with your suffering.
> Knowing the agony in Your Sacred Heart, my Love,
> my heart yearns to share this agony with You O my
> Sweet Love. What a sweet Beloved, as You lovingly
> called me, would I be, if I failed to share with You
> O most loving and sweetest of Hearts, Your agony.
>
> O that You may turn Your loving Gaze at me and have
> compassion with Your sweet beloved. Shower her with
> Your sweet love. Hold her tightly in Your loving Arms,
> press her to Your Most Sacred Heart that she may taste
> the sweet flavor of the pains in your sweetest Heart
> that turns her Heart madly in love with You. O my sweet
> Jesus I am head over heels in love with You. Help me!
>
> I belong to you body and soul, from head to toe, do
> with me as you will. May we share everything together,
> Joys and sorrows, everything, for love is for sharing.
> Love is suffering with the Beloved, my sweet Happiness.
> For You I will do anything, I love You more than myself.
> You have my will, Sweetness of my soul, Life of my soul,
> sunshine of my heart. Dearest Love, I am wholly thine.
>
> O Sweetest Love, mold me the way You want me to be
> purify me like silver and gold until You see Your Reflection
> in me. Transform me into Yourself as I am part of You. I

desire to be like You. We are kneaded together like in a
dough nothing can separate us now, O my Sweet Love,
O Love of my life, continue to beautify our love.
O how impatient I am to come home to You in Heaven. How I look forward to the Resurrection when all the fortunate souls, your Beloved Children, will be in their glorified bodies, then I will be in Your sweet loving Arms forever, my dearest Love, to always feel the sweet Flavor of Your Love throughout Eternity.

O You Who is Beauty, Who is my dream, that I may always swim in the ocean of Your Love, my sweet Prince Charming. Who my Love makes dreams come true if not You my dearest Sweet Darling. My Heaven, I adore You, most Beloved of my heart, my Hero, my Pride. Who cares about the Pomp and riches of this World? O My sweet Love You are my wealth, my most priceless Treasure.

Your Love is my luxury dearest One, I have You, I have everything. Meanwhile, my Sweet Love, keep Your watchful Gaze on me, keep me as Your exclusive personal Property and Possession forever. Sustain me with the sweetness of Your Love in this exile until the Father calls me Home, when You and Mum will come to take Your Cinderella to Your Heavenly Palace to be with You, inYou and for You eternally in Eternity – Amen.

I am indeed privileged to share with Jesus everything, joys, sorrows, sufferings, pains. On 20.12.2010, nine days after the hidden stigmata was given to me, My sweet Love made me share this painful sorrow with Him. I watched, in a dream how a priest came from the inside of his house, in the Church compound, with a boy, after some cordial greeting, he sent him off and beckoned, with a fishy smile, another boy who was waiting in the reception to come to him, both went inside. His intention was obvious. You can simply allow your imagination a free run here what must have transpired between them. When I woke up from that dream the tears of Jesus rolled down my cheeks from my eyes. I kissed them. I was deeply touched, and very sad, worried about my Sweet Love, Jesus. He has given so much and receives so little or nothing in return. We hardly pay heed to His agonized Heart. Those who hurt Him the most are His priests who are consecrated to Him. Some bad eggs that spoil the priesthood. Being a priest is not a license to Heaven. Hell is open to everyone who hardens his heart to the voice of God including priests. Let everyone seek the Lord when He can be found. Stop hurting such an infinitely merciful God. Do not forget He is also a Just God.

O Most Precious Blood of Jesus, heal the wounds in the Most Sacred Heart of Jesus Christ.

On the third of March 2012, although I know my body is the Temple of the living God and that the Holy Trinity dwells in me, yet I never felt His Heart beating in my heart, but today I did. I do not have words to express gratitude to my Jesus for His Kindness and Goodness to me unworthy though I am. That Jesus chose a wretched nothing me, less than half of an ant, to have a taste of His Divine Life in this exile, is too good to be true. I am overwhelmed and most humbled. The Heart of God beating in my heart, His perpetual habitation and tabernacle of consolation, what a wonder! I feel Him always in me. Something about God, happening around me, in me, above me, beneath me, within me, all over me is too good to be true. The Holy Trinity has made my Heart His Tabernacle. This reality, He has granted me the Grace to know and feel. This Grace enables me to speak to Jesus in my heart. He hears and responds, according to His Holy Will, to what I ask of Him. Jesus is very faithful. All that He revealed is true if we believe.

> O, Most Blessed Trinity, my God, I adore Thee.
> O Beautiful Love, wonderful sweet Love of my life.
> Today, have I discovered Thee in my inner being,
> Thine Tabernacle of consolation, my poor heart.

Within my heart pounds Thine Heart O Love Divine.
Such thrills, such excitement, such bliss, known to an
expectant mother, who for the first time the heart beat
of her baby, in her womb, doth hear. O Most Holy Trinity
Love Divine, how Thou doth Thrill me, O how I love Thee.

O Love Divine, sweet Jesus, my sweet Love, Divine
Master mine, a lonely Prisoner in the Tabernacles of
the world. Be thou consoled O my sweet Love for Thine
Prisoner of Love I be. To Thee dearest Love belongs my
heart. Thine exclusive personal property and possession.

O what delight, Divine Love is. O what sweetness, what Bliss.
How I love being loved by Thee, my sweet Love.
O how I love loving Thee my wonderful Prince charming.
Thine caresses, O sweet mystery, the thrills of Divine Love.

On 25. 03.2012 I wished I had wings to fly, so completely happy I was. It sounded like music in my ears, so sweet, so soothing, my heart so much thrilled with joy, so loving, so affectionate was the sound of the voice of my Sweet Love. His loving words sent my heart overflowing with love for Him. O how I love Jesus beyond words. After I received Him in Holy Communion, in the Eucharist, contemplating His Love for me tears rolled down my cheeks. Wondering whether the tears were mine, I heard the sweetest words my poor ears have ever heard coming from my heart "No, my sweet beloved, they are Mine" You can simply imagine how overwhelmed I was with joy, happy as a lark. Never will I forget that sweet, tender loving voice of my Sweet Love, my sweetest Jesus, the Love of my life. His tears, sweet loving tears, Pearls of great joy, Pearls of Love, how I love to kiss them, sweet kisses of my Sweet Love. O my Eternal Joy, O my Sweet Love, I'm in Heaven, Heaven is real, You are Heaven, my Love.

To have a close relationship with Jesus requires you to be yourself. Get rid of your weakness, with his help, through the Sacrament of Reconciliation. God searches the Heart, He can detect insincerity, besides, trying to be another makes you unnatural and a failure. Jesus deals with each individual in a unique way. This lesson He taught me when I found, after reading a book from a nun to whom He appeared, her approach to Him was contrary to mine. I have before this incident already established a relationship with Jesus and felt quite comfortable and happy. Our relationship was growing in beauty and sweetness. But after reading this book I became desolate, nothing could cheer me up. In fact I got confused, wondering if I was actually reaching Jesus as I thought I was doing. Thereafter, shortly before I got up from bed in the morning, on 18.4.2012, I felt some uncomfortable pressure on my chest, as though I was having a chest pain. Having had a sound sleep I could not understand the meaning of it. I got up and informed Jesus what was happening to me. It was not actually pain, but very uncomfortable. I asked Him to stop it if it was not His Holy Will. Having said that I went to the altar for my morning prayer. While in prayer I felt deep love for God in my heart realizing how deeply connected I am to Jesus, to God the Father Who has been suffering for me ever since He created me, ever since He created man. Immediately I felt I cannot be fully happy until God is happy. There is no happiness for me in this world. I realized my happiness lies in the Love of my Sweet Love, in the Love of Jesus and in loving Him. The moment I remembered His unhappiness, I became unhappy. During this contemplation the pressure on my chest disappeared immediately. It was then it dawned on me my Beloved used the uncomfortable pressure on my chest to call me down to earth. I was beginning to think I was expecting much from Him rather than allow Him to come to it Himself. God deals with each individual uniquely. He created us for Himself and for different purposes therefore, do not try to be someone else, simply be yourself and find out what He wants of you, your vocation.

X. My Mum, The Blessed Virgin

How do I start to write about Mum, my sweet darling Mum, the Blessed Virgin Mary, Mother of my Sweet Savior Jesus Christ. It is well known Jesus gave His Mother to us, making Her the Mother of every human being, consequently making us children of God the Father, brothers and sisters of Jesus. I accepted this fact, appreciated it but found it difficult to relate to Her as my mother. As I was not born into the Catholic Church, I was not used to how Catholics regard her. All the honor granted her by the Faithful was strange to me. Having been raised up in a none Catholic home, there was no devotion to Mary so, my relation to her was lukewarm. I was saying the Rosary regularly, however, without enthusiasm. It was rather a routine. One day, as I knelt down in prayer, in the afternoon, I saw, in a vision, Jesus and Mary strolling down the shore with Mary's arm round His waist and His round Hers. It appeared as though Jesus was disturbed about something and Mary was comforting Him. This gave me an insight of the intimate relationship between Jesus and His Mother. It was then I began gradually to understand the gift of Jesus, His Mother, to humanity.

I began gradually to grow in my acceptance of Mary. Thereafter, I got to know of the relationship of St. John Paul II with the Blessed Virgin. Then I thought, if he gave himself to her why should I not, after all, it is the wish of Jesus. Besides, most of the Saints I got to know loved Her very much, such as St. Louis de Monforte, so I became convinced, if I gave myself totally to Mary she would bring me closer to Her son Jesus with whom I very much longed to have a very close relationship. Having come to this conclusion, without hesitation I gave myself totally to Her asking Her to regard me as Her all – Totus tuus – like my brother, Saint John Paul II, and I began to love her. Before I knew it I discovered I have grown to love her more than my biological mother, in fact as though she bore me after Jesus. I became her little girl, her little Mary, the little sister of Jesus, after all, she is my mother. Sometimes, we weep together, sometimes we smile together, sometimes she kisses me. I feel really connected to Her. I thank God for this Grace.

> How sweet and lovely is the sweetest and
> Loveliest Lady of ladies. How beautiful is the
> Beauty of the most beautiful of all ladies, Mary
> ever Virgin. Filled with Grace, so unexampled,
> created, yet the Creators Bride she became.
>
> So was Incarnation born. Created, though she be,
> Mother of her Creator thus she became. Thus was
> born the greatest love story ever told, in it's unique,
> beauty and mystery so designed by Divine Wisdom.
> O beautiful Lady, clothed with the sun, Mother of
> God, my Savior, how dazzlingly beautiful Thou art!
> Richly endowed with the Virtues of God thy Savior,
> Divine Son Thine. O Mary my sweet Mum I love thee.
>
> O white Lily of the garden of Heavenly Delight, Queen
> of my heart, Mother most Holy, I consecrate my life to
> Thee. O Mum dear, I bid Thee my hand to take that thou
> mayst lead me, through Immaculate Heart Thine, to
> Jesus Divine Son Thine to love and cherish in my heart.
>
> O Queen of queens, Mum most dear, morning Star,
> I put my hope in Thee, O Gate of Heaven. Your cloak
> of Love my shield I make, sweet Blessed Mum mine.
> To Thee I pledge to be a loving devoted daughter.
>
> O Mother most dear, all I Thee ask, dearest sweet Mum
> mine, that my heart always be a Tabernacle of consolation,
> sweet consolation, for the Most Sacred Heart of Jesus,
> sweet Love mine, sweet Divine Son Thine. Mum I Thee love.

O Mum, most lovely of all ladies, another favor of Thee
do I ask, your worries, sweet worries, for Jesus Divine
Son Thine, Sweet Crucified Love mine, to share. O sweet
Mum, most beautiful Queen of queens, O how I love Thee.

This daughter Thine, less than half of an Ant, do give Thee
all her love. To Thee Mum most dear, as consolation, I do
pledge, to be fully joyful, in Heaven O Mum most dear, only when Jesus
fully joyful is. Then, O my sweet Queen, fully joyful will be.
Then is my Joy in Heaven complete, for the Most Sacred
Heart of Jesus, Divine Son Thine no more agony knows.

How right I was! My relationship with Jesus began to flourish. Having accepted our Lady sincerely as my Mother, my love for Her began to grow. She became my real Mum, my biological Mum, at the same time my Blessed Mum. There is nothing so comforting, so soothing and most dependable as the love of a mother. Mary my Mum became my girl-friend. Any child whose mother is his girl-friend is most favored. Jesus and Mary are inseparable therefore, to reach Jesus easily one must go through Mary who lovingly leads us to her Son. To love Jesus means loving Mary. One cannot love one without the other. The love for Jesus is incomplete if His Mother is not loved. Without Mary, no Jesus. Through her "Yes" the word became Flesh and our Redemption took place. God is pleased when we show devotion to Her. If you love your biological mother, surely you would be able to love Mary. You learn to love Her by loving your biological mother. Then transfer this love to Her, but in a greater degree, as Mary is the Mother of all humanity, without ceasing to love your biological mother. To reach Jesus love His Mother, then you have won His Most Sacred Heart, but do not fail to aim at keeping His Precepts. They are essential, to abide in His Love.

Loving the Blessed Virgin means being like Her. Are all humanity not most fortunate to have the Mother of God as their Mother? Jesus wants all humanity to be one family with Him. Therefore, loving Mary His Mother as your Mother makes Jesus your elder Brother. Unfortunately, the unbelieving heart, in the cloak of pride, no amount of lecture can convince him. The truth is, Mary is the sweetest, protective, caring, understanding, tolerant, forgiving and most loving Mother.

I would like to mention the loving gesture of the Blessed Mother during our pilgrimage to Poland early may 2012. My parish made a nine days pilgrimage to Poland. One of the important places we visited was Lichen, a city with one of the biggest Catholic Cathedrals in the world. While inside the Cathedral, my admiration of it's beauty gave my heart a pitch of joy as I felt the Majesty of God, wondering how Heaven would be. Then my longing for my Eternal Home with Jesus was aroused. Suddenly, I felt a soft tap on my shoulder by an unseen Hand. I did not need to ponder much on it as I felt it must have been an Angel. However, on leaving the Cathedral we visited the healing spring, after first visiting the monument of a wounded soldier who did not want to die in a strange land and sought the assistance of the Blessed Virgin which he received. I was not aware we would visit the healing spring so I had nothing to take some healing water with me. I felt deeply disappointed, unhappy to come from Germany to Poland, to the healing spring without taking some home with me for my children. It was actually disheartening watching others fill their bottles with the healing water. Nobody had any spare bottle and there was nowhere to buy one.

To my utter disappointment, I learnt we were not coming back there again. I had hoped to buy a bottle of mineral water drink it, and use the empty bottle to collect the holy water. Having no other alternative, I left everything at God's Mercy, telling Mum the one I drank is for all, with my heart I take some home. Just as I was leaving the place I heard someone close by calling someone else to come for a bottle. I asked if she had an extra one for me, she gave me a negative reply informing me she had already collected for herself. She wanted the person she was calling to have one. It was then I had the urge to draw nearer asking to have a look at the bottle. Taking a glance at the bottle I noticed it did not look like a bottle, besides I did not know how it could be opened. Somehow, I felt a certain urge to take it. When I took it my heart told me immediately it was meant for me. A loving gesture of my Blessed Mum who did not want her little girl to go home disappointed. On opening the beautiful portable white bottle, well designed with the image of the Blessed Virgin, as queen on one side, and Herself with the wounded soldier whose life she saved on the other side, I discovered it was filled with the healing water. Such a beautiful bottle everyone would love to have.

However, I pondered in my heart for a while, why the lady who was calling someone to come for it could not take it herself. Every Catholic Christian would love to be in possession of such a beautiful bottle. Nobody would resist the temptation of taking it. Moreover, why did the one being called not come for it. It then dawned on me it was not meant for any of them. Her call was merely to draw my attention. I was so grateful to Mum who is always there for Her children whenever they needed her most. I then remembered the tap of the Angel on my shoulder, in the Cathedral, a taste of what lay ahead for me. Thereafter, I asked my elder Brother Jesus to give Mum a kiss for me in gratitude.

On 1.2.2012, the eve of the presentation of Jesus in the Temple, I had a wonderful experience of God's special Grace. After my morning prayer, as I was making my usual salutation to Mum, the Blessed Virgin, before Her picture "Our Lady of All Nations" I felt so close to Her as never before. This was the day I first felt Her as my biological Mother. The day I felt She bore me after Jesus, my elder Brother, therefore I should love Her the way Jesus loves Her. I felt I should possess their Virtues of humility and obedience as a member of the Family. I felt very close to Her as though Her heart touched mine. It was a very intimate closeness not easy to describe. It cannot be put into words. I am very grateful to God for His Love and affection. This feeling instigated the urge to ask for the favor to love Mum the way Jesus loves Her and began regarding her as though she actually gave birth to me the natural way. But why not, after all Jesus gave Her to us as our Mother. Furthermore, we became alive when the Church was born. She is the Mother of the Church. In the new self we are biologically born of Her. All there is to it is to accept it in faith as this is a confirmed reality. Moreover, She deserves the love of all Her children. I am happy to be enclosed in the Immaculate Heart of the most loving Mother where I have taken refuge. She is my Model. A mother brings up her child to resemble his parents, so Mary my Mum brings me up to resemble Her so as to resemble My elder Brother, in order to resemble my Eternal Father, to resemble the Family and make my Beloved parents delighted in me their loving daughter.

Feeling now so close to Mum since the eve of the presentation of Jesus, when Simeon prophesied to Her a sword would pierce Her Heart, I experienced on Easter Sunday a taste of the sorrow in Mum's Heart. A touch of God's Mercy towards me His unworthy creature. The Grace of God to love His Mother the way He loves Her, though no one can ever love Her as He does, but I have been granted the Grace to love Her deeply. Although my heart has been touched by Mum in a special way, today while praying for the liberation of my sons from their emotional attachment to Anthony, for their minds to be remolded, for them to draw closer to God and open their heart for Jesus and Mary, I felt a drop of tear run down my cheek from my right eye. It tasted bitter. It was Mum's tear, as I was praying for her intercession.

It was a consolation for me, a reminder of Her sorrows, for me to know she is always there for me with Her support.

Our Lady does not want any of her children to end up in hell yet She is in sorrow due to Her fears many will, on their own freewill, that breaks Her Heart and leaves Her Divine Son in agony. Considering the ingratitude of the human heart, shown in sacrilege, contempt, dishonor, disgrace, lip service, sexual laxity, indecent clothing, to name but a few, all due to the unrequited love of the infinite Love of Her Divine Son, despite the bitter price He paid for our salvation my heart breaks. We hardly pay attention to the agony in His Most Sacred Heart and the sorrow in Her Immaculate Heart. I have given Mum all my love, I'm Her little girl, Her little Mary of the Most Sacred Heart of Jesus. I am grateful to Jesus for the Grace to love Mum as He loves Her. Mum's tear is a sign She understands my worry over my sons Emmanuel and Peter. She is on my side, all I need is patience. Jesus knows the right time suitable for His Mercy for the benefit of each soul.

When I felt Mum's love, in my heart as I stood before Her, I felt She loves me as the younger sister of Jesus. It is hard to explain. It was a wonderful feeling. I am still overwhelmed with that feeling. I felt really connected to Her, we both emotionally love each other like Mother and daughter. I was exceptionally grateful to God for this great intimacy with Mum and prayed for more such experiences with my sweet loving Blessed Mum. To my utter happiness I discovered later the first February is dedicated to the Holy Family, the presentation. I thanked God for regarding me as family. I love Jesus and Mum very very very dearly. It's a good feeling to feel belonged. Mum and Jesus are always there for their children, give them genuine love, draw close to them and they will draw close to you. They are there with wide out- stretched Arms waiting for you. Simply be yourself and be sincere, for God knows the secrets of the heart. I owe my closeness to Jesus to Mary, the Blessed Virgin, my sweet loving Mum. She has been the sweetest and dearest Mum, comforting me always, whenever I am dawn and needed Her, soothing me with Her rose scented perfume.

Mary has no rival in Her love for Jesus for nobody can love Him as She does nor be what She is to Him no matter how deep our love for Him is, it cannot be compared with the burning furnace of love in her Immaculate heart for Him. Her love for Him is exceptional. He is Her God, She is His mother, His Bride, His daughter, His friend, to mention but a few. She carried Him nine months in her womb, His first Tabernacle, nursed Him with her breast milk, and raised Him up into the most loving, obedient, beautiful, caring, compassionate and humble young Man every mother would eagerly and happily love to be hers. She held God in her arms, breast fed Him as her son, loved Him as her Savior, worshipped and adored Him as Her God, Her Spouse, Creator and Father. One can simply imagine how terribly deep the sorrow in Her Immaculate heart was as She stood and witnessed the ordeal of Her most treasured and loving son at the foot of the cross. Her Heart pierced with the sword of sorrow that nearly killed Her, dumbfounded at what became of the delicate skin of Her beautiful son, so brutally tortured, almost beyond recognition, had God not intervened and kept Her alive to sustain His young Church, that was yet to be born, She would have died of a broken heart like Her Beloved Son. So great is the love between Her and Her Divine Son, so also are Her sorrows because of Him. She understands perfectly well God's love for humanity and shares that love with Him.

The relationship between Jesus and Mary is a very deep, beautiful mystery that takes love to comprehend and only Her Spouse, the Holy Spirit can grant the Grace to comprehend it. She is the easiest means to reach the Sacred Heart of Jesus. Jesus would refuse His mother nothing. Being a Jew He has deep regard for His mother. He did not come to condemn the law but to fulfil it, He said, therefore, He is a typical Jewish Son of a typical Jewish Mother. Mary being the sweetest Mother of all draws every of Her child to His elder Brother. She is the gate of Heaven as she possesses all the virtues that please God worth emulating to touch the Heart of God. She deserves all honor. If God who is Her son honors Her who is man to do otherwise. The Almighty God is a family God. Since we already have a Father in Heaven, the Almighty God, a Mother was needed and that Mother is Mary His Mother. There is no family without a mother. At the foot of the cross, Jesus gave His mother to the beloved Apostle, the youngest of all His Apostles, allowing him represent His young Church, His mystical Body, thereby making His Mother our Mother, the Mother of the Church. He is the Vine we are the branches. Thus we became His brothers and sisters. Therefore, belong to Jesus you must belong to Mary and love Her as your Mother. To reject Mary would be rejecting the plan of the Almighty God.

It is sad for those who are misled by Satan to think Mary has other children and deny themselves the realization of the sweet, tender loving care of motherly love. Every Jew knows it would have been against the Jewish norm for someone to deny his younger brothers the right to their mother's love by giving her to another who is entirely not related to the family. That would have been an action absolutely intolerable to society and against the norms of Divine institution of family life. The simple fact is, Mary had no other children after Jesus. She remained Virgin after giving birth to Jesus. Those mentioned as brothers and sisters of Jesus were children of His Mother's sister who was also called Mary, hence there was no extra word for cousins or nephews, for the Jews every other family relation is a brother or a sister, just as it is in some parts of Africa, especially among the Ibos in Nigeria where every relation is a brother or a sister.

If Mary had other children it would have been wrong to have left them behind when they went to the Temple in Jerusalem to worship with Jesus who was then twelve years old. There was no mention of other children, but Jesus. Remember, Mary and Joseph lost Jesus and had to search for three days for Him. If there were other children, who would of course be younger than Jesus, they would have been without parents for so long, why did Mary and Joseph not feel concerned about them? Did they not deserve as much love and affection as Jesus? The fact is Mary had no other children after Jesus. Should anyone think otherwise, one should not forget our salvations enemy, the Satan, who is aware that Mary will destroy his rule with Her motherly love, he would stop at nothing to deprive God's children from embracing their Mother's love.

Mary loves each one of us as she loves Jesus. With her motherly love she draws us to Jesus. This offends Satan who sees his fate clearly, therefore he tries to deceive God's innocent children by giving them a wrong picture of God's plan, the Eternal Happiness with Him in Heaven. All that Jesus wants of us is to assist Him in His struggle for our individual salvation by uniting our crosses with His in patient obedience to His Holy Will, ask for the Grace to persevere. It is only for a while to inherit everlasting life, eternally in His Glory. It is easy, with His Grace, if you will it. That is, if Heaven is your goal. Everyone who believes that Jesus is the Christ is a child of God, and everyone who loves the parent loves the child. 1 Jn 5 vs 1 Mary is the Parent, Jesus the Child. Jesus and Mary are one, they cannot be separated.

XI. The Beloved in the Eucharist

The Passover, Jewish religious celebration commemorating their deliverance from Egypt, a feast of joy which leaves a feeling of belonging to Yahweh, God of their patriarchs, their God, the only God Who liberated them from slavery with a mighty Hand. This God was their pride, their God who they saw as their possession. The feast of Passover became a communion whereby their gratitude to the one and only God, the Almighty God, for all His benefits, was expressed. A feast of thanksgiving to the Almighty God when a lamb without blemish is killed and consumed.

Now a more greater communion with God was yet to be instituted, a communion whereby this Almighty God would be shared by everyone, regardless of race, ruling out the possessiveness of the Jews as the only nation with the right to reach this one and only God. A communion that would embrace all of human kind uniting them into a family, as was intended at the creation of man, with God as their Father. This communion, a new covenant, was to overshadow the Passover and also a lamb was to be killed and consumed. This time this lamb would be the Son of God, God Himself.

"For God so loved the world, that he gave his only son, that whoever believes in him should not perish but have eternal life." When the time was ripe, on the feast of Passover, the Lamb of God instituted the more greater communion and offered His Body and Blood as food and drink to give man life in Himself, for man to share His Divine life with Him.

A wonderful, beautiful act of God that portrays His infinite love for man for which man would never be able to be grateful enough. Humanity would never be able to express enough appreciation for this wonderful noble deed of God that surpasses human comprehension. In one of His regular admonishing speeches Jesus stated clearly the meaning of the communion He intended to institute. "I am the living bread which came down from heaven; if any one eats of this bread, he will live forever; and the bread which I shall give for the life of the world is my flesh....Truly, truly I say to you, unless you eat the flesh of the son of man and drink his blood, you have no life in you; he who eats my flesh and drinks my blood has eternal life, and I will raise him up at the last day. For my flesh is food indeed, and my blood is drink indeed. He who eats my flesh and drinks my blood abides in me, and I in him. As the living Father sent me, and I live because of the Father, so he who eats me will live because of me. This is the bread which came down from heaven, not such as the fathers ate and died; he who eats this bread will live forever." Jn 6 vs. 51 – 58

During the celebration of the feast of Passover Jesus replaced it with the Eucharist, when He offered His body and Blood as food under the appearances of bread and wine, a sacramental expression of the Easter mystery which He asked His Apostles to celebrate always, in memory of Him. Consequently He ordained and authorized them, as Priests, in His Person, in Persona Christi, to evoke the Almighty Father for the transubstantiation of the bread and wine into His Blood and Body and give Him to others, as He has given Himself to them. A manifestation of His love for humanity for whose salvation He gave His life in sacrifice. This is how Jesus instituted the priesthood through whose consecrated hands He would be shared among us. Thus the Eucharist, which is Jesus Himself, Body, Blood, Soul and Divinity, replaces the Passover. Jesus became the sacrificial Lamb, sinless, taking upon Himself the load of sin, died to save man from sin and reinstate man in his sinless nature possessing God's virtue of Humility, obedience and love, acquired through transformation, from the consummation of the Lamb of God in the Holy Eucharist, to worship, adore, praise and love God his Creator, consequently be showered with the love of God His Father. This Mystery, vaguely comprehended by the human mind will be fully comprehended in Eternity in God's Glory.

God's love for humanity is a Mystery to be solved by Jesus in Eternity. However, to some chosen of God, a glimpse into this beautiful Mystery has ben granted in order to rouse in man the desire to strive to abide in God's love by keeping His Precepts and ultimately share in His Glory in Eternity. Jesus desires all humanity to abide in His Love so as to live in Him, with Him and for Him in His Glory. The Eucharist is an essential Sacrament He desires all to partake.

However, it is most unfortunate, that this gift of God of Himself is hardly appreciated. Sometimes, watching the nonchalant attitude with which most people receive Jesus in the Eucharist, in their hands, as though they are receiving a piece of biscuit handed to them by an acquaintance, without genuflecting, makes one sad. Why not show respect, acknowledge the presence of the Almighty God, Creator of Heaven and Earth, Author and Giver of life, the Great I AM and approach Him with respect and awe. Why not receive Him with love, Who in His infinite Mercy, for love of you, humbled Himself and remains for you in the Tabernacle, so as to nourish your soul with Himself to enable you become like Him and share His Divine Life with Him. The heavenly Host praise and worship Him without ceasing. Normally, Humanity should tremble before Him, but He does not even ask for that, but that His love should be reciprocated. In humility He is there in all the Tabernacles of the world twenty-four hours every day, one hardly pay attention to Him.

Do not allow Satan blind you. Jesus is truly present in the Eucharist and in the Tabernacle. If you received Him in a state of Grace, and open your heart for Him, Jesus Who is a generous God would surely show you His appreciation. Jesus promised He was not going to leave us as orphans, He did not. He is in the Tabernacle in every Catholic Church. What a wonderful gift of God to adorn us with His Divine Presence, a Prisoner of Love in our Tabernacles. It would be very unwise to take God's love for granted.

Jesus desires to be received in the mouth. One can understand that, especially in this times when His Love is taken for granted. This would encourage awe and respect for Him, instigating in us the consciousness of His Greatness, His Majesty and Holiness. His reception in the hand, with time, makes Him common. It becomes a routine. It reduces the reverence due to Him consequently, causing the feeling of familiarity that breeds contempt. This is wrong. There is no doubt this is the main factor of the scarcity of priests and consecrated vocations in most countries where this practice is extreme. Only very few people have the courage to voice it out. The Bishops, who are His Apostles should see to the Holy Will of their Divine Master. They should see that catechists catechize children on receiving Jesus in the mouth to instill awe of God in them. This will eventually enable them be aware of God's Love, encourage them as they grow to reciprocate God's Love for them. After the transubstantiation every particle becomes Jesus therefore, for young communicants or adults to receive Him in one hand, using the other hand to put Him in the mouth, whereby particles are disposed of, by robbing of hands on clothes or on other objects, is very disrespectful. This carelessness definitely displeases the Lord. Let love rule the heart to nourish virtues which enhance the soul, through Grace, for God's Love.

> O Desire, sweet desire, that hunts my heart.
> How long will you leave me hungering for the
> kisses from my Beloved. Dearest Love, Life
> and Light of my soul, come O sweet Love to
> Your sweet beloved. My soul yearns for the
> sweet nectar in the flavour of your Love.
>
> O living Host, sweet Love of mine, hasten to
> your sweet beloved, satisfy the desires in my
> heart, fill me with your warmth, with your kisses,
> with sweet caresses of Your tender Love, that

sends my heart on fire, soaring on high, filled with love for You O sweet beautiful Love so Divine.

Thus Your Soul unites with mine more tightly in the bond of love, O Most Blessed Eucharistic Food, nourishment of my soul. Sweet Sacrament of Love, Most Holy Most Divine, I adore and I love Thee Profoundly. O sweet beautiful Love, how I love Thee.

The Eucharist is the source and summit of the Catholic Faith. The greatest gift God gave me is the Grace to be Catholic. This has enabled me get to know the God who created me is within reach, much closer than I ever imagined. Being Catholic has enabled me be part of His Family, share in the wealth of Her Faith and enjoy the benefits of the Sacraments. O What a blessing it is to belong to the Holy Roman Catholic Church, to the One, Holy, Catholic and Apostolic Church founded by Jesus Christ Himself. The Magisterium of the Catholic Church has no rival and nothing surpasses Her Beauty and Holiness because Her Founder is God and He is Holy. It does not matter whether Her members are sinners or not, She is Holy because the Holy Spirit is Her Soul. To belong to Her is to possess a priceless Treasure to be most treasured, cherished, and loved. She is Jesus. Therefore, knowing and practicing the Catholic Faith is a must. She is a sure passage to Heaven therefore, a privilege to belong to Her as She possesses the Sacraments for sanctifying Grace. Jesus came to give life to humanity, this He does through His Church enriched in Sacraments for Eternal Glory, for a life with Him in Him and for Him.

Born an Anglican, tossed here and there and out of His Mercy, at the time I thought I had lost Him, He found me, embraced me and gave me the Catholic Faith. Satan tried every devilish means to deprive me of it, but God in His infinite Goodness gave me victory and the Grace to embrace His Love. Every Christian can actually find fulfilment in the Catholic Faith where He left us all the seven Sacraments for a fulfilled

Christian life. Most Catholics do not really realize what they have in their Catholic Faith. A wealthy knowledge of the Catholic Faith is essential for every Catholic in order to be equipped to withstand the danger of deviating into the bondage of sectarianism where the ears of members are tickled with fables to betray in deepest consequence. Jesus founded a Church with His Apostles.

He did not come to abolish the law but to fulfil it therefore, just as the kings of Israel used to have prime ministers who held the keys of their kingdom, regulated the affairs of the state in the absence of the king, in the same way Jesus chose Peter, changed his name, transferred His own name "Rock" to him and gave Him the keys of the kingdom of Heaven. Peter therefore became His Vicar, the visible Head of His Holy Church. Jesus did not found Churches, but only one Church and He desires His Church to be one just as He is one with His Father. This He made known in His famous prayer in John's gospel chapter 17. The Jesus who made this prayer is still the same. He is God and He does not change. It was never His desire that there should be reformation which took place in the 16th century resulting to the splitting of the Church to give rise to the establishment of reformed, protestant churches. The enemy planted the weeds, He advised they should be left to grow with the wheat until the Harvest when the Angels will do the harvesting.

God is a triune God, united in Himself, the Holy Trinity. The Church, the Mystical Body of Christ, is the Vine, Her members are the branches therefore, they must be united as the body cannot be divided. It must be called to mind that Jesus himself said the gate of hell will not prevail against His Church. God keeps His word. Heaven and earth must pass away but not God's word. Jesus is strictly against disunity. Jesus being God, aware of what would take place in His Church, in His absence, knowing the human weakness, warned His members against the enemy with the parable of the tares, the weeds. It is not a man's place to pass judgement, which is for God. The Reformationists disobeyed God, the disobedience resulted in thousands of sectarian churches all over the world, each claiming to be operating through the Holy Spirit. If truly they are operating through the Holy Spirit why still the disunity? One must never forget what Jesus said about the blind leading the blind, for both will fall into the pit.

If there is a sincerity to worship and serve God, then there is the need to serve Him the way He wants to be served and not the way we want to serve Him. He set a pattern by which He should be worshiped, adored and praised therefore, otherwise, would be a waste of time. When Jesus instituted the priesthood, on the eve of His passion, during the first celebration of the Holy Eucharist, the first Mass, when He ordained His Apostles priests, authorized them to continue to celebrate the Mass, the breaking of the Bread, He did so because He does not desire His passion and Resurrection to get into forgetfulness. They are to be continuously celebrated until He comes. He distinctively demonstrated His intention of being represented by male priests only, so He did not ordain any female priest nor did He choose any female among the 12 Apostles. As there was no woman among His Apostles, therefore, no woman is authorized to consecrate the bread and wine. We are dealing with the Most Holy and perfect Will of the Almighty God, the Creator of Heaven and Earth, the Author and Giver of life, not with a politician on a political platform.

God is Holy and those who worship Him must worship Him in truth and in holiness. It is true God is Love and patient, but we should not forget He is also a righteous Judge. He would not compel any one to love Him yet He would appreciate it if His Love is reciprocated. Every individual has the opportunity of a choice until His second coming which is fast approaching. Now is the time to embrace His Divine Mercy, accept Him as He is and not try to change Him.

At moment Jesus is using every means to draw the attention of all the human race to the danger in paying a deaf ear to His voice. He is a Merciful God ready to forgive every genuinely repentant sinner, even the worst sinner. Everyone should approach Him without fear for He is Love. He has revealed to us His Merciful Heart through St. Faustina therefore, every sinner should run away from the enticement of Satan. He is wickedness and death. Accept the invitation of Jesus who is Love and Life. Do not delay to accept God's Mercy, time is running out, His second coming is fast approaching, be wise. The Divine Mercy is for the preparation of His second coming. Do not be taken by surprise. He came that we might have life and have it more abundantly. Abide in His Love, keep His commandments for His Joy to be in you, so that your joy may be full. His Yoke is light, all it needs is a strong will for a "Yes."

During my time as Anglican, I did not experience God's love as I do now. That left me wondering if the Anglican Communion is actually Jesus Himself. There is a danger here, should there not be any transubstantiation, I'm afraid they must be receiving just ordinary bread and wine. Jesus said one must eat His flesh and drink His Blood in order to have life. If Jesus is not being received, then make hay while the sun shines, go back home to the Catholic Church. Jesus will be very happy to welcome every sheep that comes back to the flock with wide opened Arms. This is His desire that we should all be under one Flock. "All that the Father gives me will come to me; and him who comes to me I will not cast out. For I have come down from heaven, not to do my own will, but the will of him who sent me; and this is the will of him who sent me, that I should lose nothing of all that he has given me, but raise it up at the last day. ... Do not murmur among yourselves. No one can come to me unless the Father who sent me draws him; and I will raise him up on the last day. It is written in the prophets, 'And they shall all be taught by God" Jn 6 vs 37 – 45.

However, to be just simply Catholic is not a key to Heaven. Faith without work is dead, but to be a practicing Catholic is a key to heaven. The Catholic Faith has all the Sacraments instituted by Jesus Himself for sanctification of the soul. If only Catholics would wake up and practice their Faith, appreciate the richness of their Faith it would be a help for other denominations to cross the bridge of segregation and be united with their brothers and sisters under one Flock. The bad eggs among the priests should realize the privilege of being Jesus, stop soiling the Holy priesthood. They should stop disgracing Jesus. Their aim should be to resemble Jesus therefore, they should spend time with Him in the Tabernacle. They should practice having Holy hours with Him to draw strength and receive Grace for what they lack.

Why not emulate St. Paul and put flesh under subjection. God is all powerful and there is nothing He cannot do so why not seek His assistance in His real presence. The all-powerful God is there with you in the Church. Do not forget what Jesus Himself said about waywardness, causing any of these young ones who believe in Him to go astray "better for that man for a mill stone to be hung on his neck and he be cast into the sea" To be a priest is not a guarantee for Heaven, it all depends on how passionate a priest is with his vocation. It is important to observe adoration hours in parishes on weekly or monthly basis, where possible, on daily basis for priestly vocations, for religious life and personal needs. We have the Almighty God in our midst, the silent Beloved, a prisoner of love in our Tabernacles, let us make good use of this wonderful opportunity we have while we can. God is there waiting for us to visit Him. The patient Beloved, lonely in the Tabernacle waiting for the visit of His loved ones.

XII. God the Father

Have you ever considered what it all entails calling God "Our Father" or is it simply a habit because Jesus taught us to do so? Do you take God's love for granted or do You realize He is truly your Father? What I am driving at is that children have a duty towards their fathers and so do fathers towards their children. On 8.11.2011 pondering in my heart on God's love for us, at the love of Jesus for us, not because we are human beings, but because we are His children, I was deeply moved. He has proved Himself a Father indeed, giving us unfathomable love, caring and protecting us to the point of sacrificing and risking everything for our salvation. But what have we given Him, nothing, mostly lip service. He is mostly remembered when difficulties arise. As soon as the difficulties are overcome He gets into oblivion. God the Father plays His role as Father unexceptionally well, but do you play your role as children well enough? Those who are parents themselves should consider how they would feel if their children disregarded them, if they payed little or no attention to them, doing whatever they wanted. If they disregarded their parental authority, would that not cause their hair grow grey? But God, the Almighty Father, tenderly pleads with you to turn to Him despite your unworthiness. Jesus is tenderly warning you, protecting you from the danger that lies ahead if you paid no heed to His call. He warns you against the deceitful enemy of humanity, Satan, who has nothing, but perdition to offer you.

Jesus paid a bitter price with His Divine Life for your salvation. If there was no danger there would not have been any need for the good Lord to undergo such terrible torture on His Blessed Body. Jesus treasures the life of His beloved children more than His own Life therefore, He gave it up in obedience to His Father and found it worth it. But what has He got in return from His beloved children to whom He gave all His love, nothing, but unrequited love. Unrequited love is most heart-rending.

Why not wake up from slumber, realize your Beloved Heavenly Father is troubled. Why not assist Jesus realize His Vision quickly, save Him from more agony for your eternal joy.

Yes, Jesus has conquered the powers of darkness, but He still has to conquer the hearts of all His children. He has won our salvation, the power of original sin has been destroyed, the gates of Heaven opened for humanity, but the little left, individual struggle for salvation, appears to be a thorn in the flesh for those blinded by Satan with the pomp and riches of this world. Such are God's children who cause Him Agony in His Sacred Heart with their lukewarm love. While I pondered over all this in my heart, realizing how He must be feeling I asked Him to take care of Himself. Having said that, I became aware He is the Great I AM, the all Powerful God, Lord of Heaven and Earth, Author and Giver of life and realized how tiny I am, less than half of an ant, I thought I was wrong to advise Him. At once His Tears rolled down my cheeks. Then I realized how sad Our Heavenly Father must be, how much He needs His children to return Love for love. I was deeply moved. God loves humanity. They are His children. He has life in His Hands for His children. Satan is out to destroy God's children, but God wants to snatch them away from him. Why not chose life and live. Please realize this world is transitory. Everything passes away, be not deceived, accept the Father's infinite Love. Our Heavenly Father is Almighty, He would have dealt with Satan, the coward, but He waits fore more souls to be saved.

I decided to love God in a special way as He has never been loved before, yes, somehow differently, to remain His child, His little girl, loving Him with the heart and mind of a child. One day Jesus asked me to write down my feelings for him. As I was contemplating on God's love for humanity I realized He must have feelings like us having created us in His image. There must be times when He is happy and times when He is sad. Therefore, as our Father He must expect us to consider His feelings just as we do to our biological parents. A parent appreciates it when his child observes his moods and inquires about his well-fare. Every loving child cares about the health of his parents and looks for the comfort of his parents. A child, for instance, never tolerates insults or attack on his parents, he immediately puts up a defensive attitude, on impulse, without considering the power of the attacker. Although the child may not be strong enough to challenge the attacker, but his gesture at defending his parents portrays his love for them and his parents are pleased. God wants to be loved this way also. He yearns for His children's affection and wants to be honored, respected and loved like a family member because He is the Father of all, including our parents.

In the course of my contemplation I remembered how much I loved my biological father and realized the love I had for him was meant for God, but in a greater degree because He is my real Father and the Father of my biological father. My father was acting as father, being physically present, representing my Father who is invisible, the Almighty God. My biological father was my guardian therefore, I should shower God with the love I gave to my father, in a greater degree. I felt that God, my real Father, deserves the love of His daughter that I am. He loves me unfathomably therefore, I should look for His comfort, give Him less worry by doing His Most Holy and Perfect Will. I should draw close to Him Who is ever loving and caring, longing to hold me in His Arms and fill me with Love. I should trust Him like a baby in it's mother's arms because a Father that loves me so infinitely will always desire what is best for me. He is worthy of my trust. I decided never to be a source of worry for my Most Sweet Beloved Heavenly Father any more.

> Almighty God, ever loving Father, I pray
> thee, remove in me all that offend thee I
> pray Thee, replace them with all that please
> Thee. Grant me, I beseech Thee the Grace
> To grow deeper and deeper in love with Thee.

May I be consumed with passion of love for
You. Dear Holy Spirit my God, teach me how
to console Jesus. Teach me Things I do not
know, things I should know so as to always be
a source of great delight to the One Holy and
indivisible Holy Trinity, my God Whom I adore.

My Jesus, may I be useful to You according
to Your Holy Will. May we always walk together,
Work together holding hands. The desire of
Your Most Sacred Heart is my hearts desire.

O how I do desire that sinners be saved. May
atheists give You their hearts. May they realize
what a wonderful loving Father You are. May
their blindness be healed that They may see.

O that atheist may realize their own self is a sure
proof of Your existence. Your Wonderful Beautiful
Creation speak of You, praise the splendor and
the exclusive Sovereignty of Your Divine Wisdom.

O Father Divine, You desire all Your children to be
Saints. Strengthen and encourage me, keep me from
sin. Take me by the hand, lead me safely into Your
Arms in Heaven, that I may rest on Your Most wonderful
Most loving, Most Beautiful fatherly Bosom in Eternity,
and love You eternally as your darling daughter.

Keep me under Your personal protection Dad, transform me into Mercy. Infuse in me Mum's Virtues to
resemble Jesus, my Love, on whose Holy Cross I have
crucified self, that I may resemble You, for I am Family.

Grant me more than I ask, I implore You Dad. You are my Dad. You know all I need, that I might please You – Amen!

Oh, the total giving of self to the Beloved, the union of two souls, the Lover and the beloved in complete surrender to the bond of love is the most fulfilling. I realize I am on the way to Heaven, experiencing in a most special way, my Sweet Love, a way known to lovers only. No effort of mine was needed to excel to heights my little mind would never have imagined possible. This flavor of love from my Beloved still thrills me as I go about my daily activities. How delightful it is for a soul to be desired in reciprocation to a faithful love. I have absolute confidence in the love of Jesus for me. He will never abandon me. O it is most overwhelming the realization the Holy Trinity, my God, Jesus, my Sweet Love, could lower Himself, in my nothingness, wretchedness and unworthiness, to my level, granting me, a nonentity, the sweet Flavor of His Most Divine Love, uniting intimately with me, a nobody, a Cinderella. O Most Sacred Heart of Jesus, Most sweetest Heart of Jesus I belong to You and to You alone my one and only Love.

My sibling and I were blessed with very humble loving parents. My father, some people say, was humility itself. He left us with the biggest inheritance a father could leave for his children, Jesus. As already mentioned, my father was not Catholic, but became one just before the Lord called him Home, when he said "yes" to my request to worship with me in the Catholic Church, as it would make me happy if we had the same Faith. Thereafter, he requested I should come home for Christmas that year. But due to the circumstances that prevailed, already mentioned, I was unable to make it. He went back to God, his Father, on the 29th December 2006. The Lord had Mercy and gave him the opportunity to say "Yes" before his departure. My father later appeared to me, in a dream, looking very young, smart, and radiant, this was the man who went to his Savior at the age of 91, and gave me a kiss. My youngest sister,

Evelyn, was in the room with me but she did not see him. All I could say to him was simply "I thought you have left." It was his way of saying "Thank you" to me for insisting he should be Catholic. Today, he is in Heaven by Jesus whom he loved very dearly.

His great love for Jesus instigated him to instruct us all, his children, to make Heaven at all cost. Jesus said, all that the Father has given Him no one will take away from Him. He has a way of reaching out to those who are His, including those outside His Holy Church, provided it is not through their own fault. My father belongs to the uncanonized saints having lived a saintly life. My aim is to love God the way He has never been loved before, remain a child and love Him with the heart of a child more than I loved my father. Funny though it may sound, I was born on September twenty-three 1949, although my identity card and passport bear 1951, two years younger, a childish folly, not wanting to be regarded older than friends of the same age who reduced their age. Despite that, I did not grow up. I remained the teenage girl her parent dote on. This is God's Mercy. It enables me feel like a child at heart in dealing with God the Father, loving Him as though He is my biological Father and so much more. Loving Him with the heart of a child, as His little girl, His darling daughter, His little Mary of the Most Sacred Heart of Jesus makes it my duty to protect His interest Who is my Father. Honestly, I am thrilled, excited to be the child of the Almighty God! What a privilege!

Human beings are created to learn to love God by first learning to love their biological parents. Look at me, at the age of sixty-two I feel like a nineteen years old. I believe God purposely left me that way. I went through many waters in this exile. An object of amusement for Satan and his agent who spurned me, spat at me, called me a fool, parasite, scourged me, called me a slave, he cannot respect me, I was not his wife. Indeed I was not his wife, thanks to God's Mercy, for light and darkness have nothing in common, besides his tongue nullified it all. Marriage is a union between two united souls. They are no more two but one, in

God. It is a union between man and woman and God. A triune affair which is inseparable according to God's Holy Will. Today, Jesus has healed me, saved me, fills me with His Love. I am in His Arms and His Most Sacred Heart is my Refuge. I am the bride of God, out of His infinite Mercy.

I have such great sympathy for God the Father Who has been suffering ever since He created Man, double-crossed by Satan which has been causing Him great sorrow. It is not a big deal for God to get rid of him completely, destroy the world and create another, but He has a principle how He functions. God is Goodness and Love He does not take back what He has given except when there is no other choice, in order to stop evil and enhance good. To realize God's love for man is not because man is a human being, but simply because He created him in His image, gave him all His love, so, man is His child, gave me an insight of God's dilemma. He has been trying to gather His children lovingly the way a hen gathers its broods with so much heart-ache.

There is nothing He has not done for His children and there is nothing He would not do for them to return love for love. God, the Almighty Father, left His Heavenly Throne, without minding the risk, only to be insulted, humiliated, terribly tortured, mocked, spat at, scourged, crowned with thorns, beaten with iron rods on the wreath of thorns upon His Sacred Head, by his children, all these and more He subjected Himself for you and me. What else do you expect from Him to realize how much He loves you? When will you wake up O man to assist your Heavenly Father in His loving efforts to give you life. If you drew nearer to Him you would realize Heaven here on earth, you will know Him better. He loves you more than your biological father does. You will feel at home by God, your Father. He yearns to give you love, to help you please Him and live with Him eternally in Eternity.

XIII. My way of loving God the Father

Remember, Satan is your enemy not your friend, a very crafty devil, enticing God's children with the lust, pomp and riches of this world. He is the enemy of God, your Father who loves you with infinite love. Do you realize the more you sin, by paying heed to Satan's enticement, you are supporting your Father's enemy against your Father and against yourself? Do you realize you would be making yourself a laughing stock for Satan who regards you as an imbecile. The moment you begin to realize God is your Father, not just a mere word, but with conviction, you will begin to fall in love with Him, loving Him as a child loves his father, but more because you will then realize He deserves it being the Father of us all including your biological father. You will then find your life, have peace and equilibrium.

As you know, for me God the Father is my Father whom I love as I loved my biological father but more. I love Him the way a daughter loves her father and I aim at pleasing Him and desire His happiness more than I do mine. Sometimes I inquire to know how He feels, realizing He must be expecting His children care about His feelings. Knowing I cannot be able to do anything for Him, but to love Him, I felt He would appreciate it if I asked. The consciousness of His feelings enables me aim at keeping His commandments, with love, which makes them seem easy being borne with love. There is nothing love cannot do if it is real. I walk with God the Father on father daughter relationship basis. It works for me. It will work for you if you tried, if you are sincere, because He is your Father too.

During the Nigerian Biafra civil war, at a certain time schools reopened in some areas not affected by the war, at the time, so I went back to school putting up with a girl-friend. One day, my father, who was used to going places in his car now came to see me on a bicycle looking very thin, having recovered from an illness. When I saw him my heart was very much touched. I was full of compassion for him, so much concerned, feeling sorry he had to ride all the way on bicycle just to see how I was doing. Remembering this incident my compassion was aroused for God, the Almighty Father, Creator of Heaven and Earth. My Father Who has loved me unfathomably ever before He created me. His mere thought to create is love. Everything He did and does is love flowing out from the ocean of His Divine Mercy, seeking for my love, He emptied out Himself. I was deeply moved, almost reduced to tears. If only we could put God in our hearts, in the place of our fathers we would begin to realize His suffering for our waywardness. Then we would begin to have real compassion for Him Who has been suffering ever since He created man. Then we would begin to understand gradually the pain in God's Heart, being deprived of the love of His children. Just as His Love for humanity and the ocean of His Divine Mercy are unfathomable, so also the agony in His Heart as Father.

My wonderful Most Beloved Heavenly Father, I love you with all my heart, strength, mind and soul. I desire to remain always your loving daughter, the apple of your eye. I want to remain always your child, Your little girl, Your little Mary of the Most Sacred Heart of Jesus, Your princess, Dad's darling. I did not grow up, I am still a child, your darling daughter. I love you with the heart and mind of a child. Please Father, accept my gratitude for Jesus Who has given me His love and whom I love passionately. He emptied Himself out for love of me, my heart belongs to Him. My heart shall know no other love. I belong to Him body and soul, from head to toe. All that I am belong to Him. To Him I surrender entirely all, stripping myself of all the ties to the things of this world whose fate is transient. I desire that He possesses me and works out His Holy Will for me. May I be completely one with Him as He is one With you my sweet Beloved Heavenly Father. All that you gave Him He returned back to You to be one with You, in the same manner sweetest Father, all that He has given me I return back to Him to be completely one with Him as

He is with You. Most Merciful Beloved Father, grant that I may always do Your Holy Will so that You will always be delighted with me when You look at me. Thank You for creating me. Thanks for being there for me. I am excited You are my Father. I am proud of You Dad – Amen!

Everyone needs love, so does God the Father. He created us in His own image, so He needs love and attention from His children. Consider little children celebrating the birthday of their parents or during Christmas when presents are exchanged, who, having no financial means of their own, joyfully would make some drawings, as present for their parents. Think of the joy in their parents hearts, who, perhaps expected nothing from them, yet thrilled with joy for the loving thoughts of their children. God the Father is not different. The little things we do for Him with love is much appreciated. Our Heavenly Father has everything, He lacks nothing but the love of His children. It is very sad. He needs the love and affection of His children on whom He lavishes love and affection. The Almighty God would be delighted if you showed Him you love Him too. In little things think of God always. Pay attention to Him in prayer, express your love and affection to Him. Mean all you say to Him. Keep your Heavenly Father happy by doing His Holy Will. Surrender to Him in love. Let Him know you depend on Him. Thank Him for His favors unworthy though you are.

A personal relationship with God the Father is advisable. Try loving Him with the Heart and mind of a child. Then you will begin to love and appreciate Him in Jesus Christ, the second Person of the Trinity, as the Holy Spirit grants you the Grace to see Him with the eyes and mind of a child, while you love Him with the heart of a child. In so doing you will be able to realize the Father's agony, His thirst for the love of His children. When the Father's agony is recognized, then would every of His children do all in his or her power to seek the source of His agony. Once this is discovered then the urge for the remedy would be there. He is more than willing to grant you the Grace to overcome your weaknesses if you asked Him. Then the tears in the eyes of God, our Father, would dry up. Imagine the Almighty God shedding tears because of you and me. What a loving Father. Let us stop sin and hurt God no more. He is the best Father. All it takes is patience, perseverance, obedience in humble trust, surrendering your will to Him.

Moreover, every child defends his father from his attacker. He always takes side for his father against his enemies. During my childhood, I was a quiet girl, not used to much words, but the only time I had courage to challenge anyone was when someone insulted or shouted at my humble parents who would not want to exchange words with them. That is the instinct of every child who loves his parents. The Almighty Father is your Father, therefore, you should not keep silent, watching Satan take advantage of His weakness, His love for you and allow yourself to be snatched away from your Heavenly Father for perdition. Do you not realize that going against the Heavenly Father's Will you choose side with the enemy of your Father, Satan. In so doing you choose death at will. Jesus has made known to man the Father's infinite Love and His great desire to give man eternal life. Give the Father the love that rightly belongs to Him. He is good. Let Satan be put to shame. He is your arch enemy, the father of liars. You are on his side when you commit sin. You hurt yourself and offend God your Father. Satan hates you and desires to see you in hell to hurt God.

Trust in God He is your Father. He loves you. He will never fail you. Jesus gave us wonderful Sacraments. A regular reception of the sacrament of penance helps to avoid sin and to get rid of bad habits. Do not wait for a year or more as some Catholics do. The urge to remain always under the state of Grace encourages one to be aware of the enemy, Satan. It instigates one to receive this Sacrament as often as possible. We have a sweet loving Father, love Him.

I have grown to trust God the Father like a baby in its mother's arms. For God the Father, all humanity are His children. His little children. It does not matter how old or how young you are, you are His child therefore, be the child you are, a loving child, His little child and enjoy your Heavenly Father. Has He not done enough for you? Have pity on your Beloved Father Who has been revealed to you by Jesus Christ. Acting otherwise, is hurting yourself and being against yourself. Do not be deceived by Satan, overcome him by the power of your Father the way Jesus did when He was tempted of the devil. The devil cannot tempt you „above that you are able" Do not take the Father's love for granted. Do not simply assume, He is my Father, He loves me infinitely. He is Merciful. That would be a big mistake. Yes, He loves you infinitely and He is Merciful, but have you requited His love and kept His commandments? Are you merciful? Love is a two way traffic, give and take. The lover expects to be loved, then is the equation balanced, both are pleased. Show God you love Him by keeping His commandments. He always grants a helping hand if efforts are sincere. The fact God created man in His own image makes it quite natural that He should expect you to care for His feelings as you care for the feelings of your biological father. After all, are you not expected to learn to love God through loving your biological father? Humanity owe Him complete dependency and love as their Father, the Author and Giver of life.

When a child misbehaves his father reprimands him because he loves his child. He wants to embed good social morals in him. The Almighty Father reprimands His children also in like manner when they go astray because he loves them. If He did not care He would not bother. I do not know if you realized, that when you are reprimanded by the Eternal Father He feels it more than you do? He would have preferred there was no need for the Cross. The Cross is there, therefore, everyone has to bear it with love for our Lord Jesus Christ Who bore the greatest of it. Of course, it is the Father's desire you would understand His Love for you, recognize Him as Father, return Love for love, not lip service, then there would be no need for reprimand. He wants you to resemble Him. He is Love. You are made by Love, for Love and with

Love so, you should be Love. A child takes after his parents. Your Parents, Jesus and Mary are Love, you should be Love. From Love flows Mercy. If you are perfected in love you will become mercy, love and mercy like God the Father Who is Love and Mercy. For this reason God is transforming humanity, His children to be as He is. Heaven is Love, one who does not have Love is not fit for Heaven so, give God the chance to transform you.

Sometimes, you feel down or dispirited at His silence when you need something from Him. You would have been delighted to have Him grant you every request instantly, but which father in whose heart lies the interest of his child does that. Have you considered you might be asking for something which might not be beneficial to your spiritual life, to your relationship with Him? It could be painted, in your eyes by Satan, to be very essential for you, but God knowing you better than you know yourself, refrains from granting it or delays it to grant it when it would be best for you.

Consider a child, who needed a bicycle, his father could not afford it at once for financial reasons, but the child was unaware of his father's indisposition. All he wanted was the bicycle. He repeatedly demanded it from his father because his friend had one. His father, deeply touched, unhappy over his financial incapability to meet up with the demand of his son, who thought his father could afford everything, could not explain to his son the reason he has not purchased him the bicycle yet. His son was made a laughing stock by his friend for not being able to possess a bicycle. This coupled with his unawareness of his father's helplessness broke his heart. He felt his father did not love him. If the boy's father could have helped it, he would have met up with his son's demand and so saved his son's face from his friend. This is exactly how it is with God the Father and humanity, His children. He feels sad when we are sad. He would have given us everything for the asking, but that would not be love. He is making us to be in conformity with Him to share His

Divine Life with Him. He cannot change Himself. He is the Great I AM. He is. He wants to burn out our sinful nature to enable us take up His nature, Love. He wants to see the reflection of Himself in us in order to have pleasure in us as His children. His silence is Love. He gives us what will not sour our belly. It is good to give Him absolute confidence for He knows what is good for us. The child asking his father for a bicycle did not know how much his father was suffering for not being able to afford it right away to please him. God wants us to love Him for Himself, to open our hearts to Him, and see Him as Father.

In order to be the child of the Father, loving Him with the heart and mind of a child, protecting His interest, I do the following:

1. I submitted myself totally to His Holy Will.
2. I put my complete trust in Him.
3. I became the Father's child.
4. I renounced Satan.
5. I love the Father with all my mind, strength, heart and soul.
6. I despise Satan with all my mind, strength, heart and soul.
7. I love the Father with the heart and mind of a child.
8. I believe all that Jesus himself revealed, through His saints and through His Holy Church.
9. I do not ask question, if at all, only to enhance the beauty of my love for Him and not to find why He did or did not do, God cannot deceive, I simply believe. Unnecessary questioning is for me irrelevant, all that matters is how to make Heaven and swim in the ocean of His love.
10. I am watchful of the enemy, the Satan.
11. I avoid questioning and simply believe as I realized questioning calls for doubts if understanding is not reached, and that creates room for the enemy to poke his nose.
12. I realized in my heart and soul I am God's child.
13. I believe in His unfathomable Love for me.

14. I aim at protecting the Father from Satan by despising what Jesus despises and loving what He loves.
15. I show God the Father I am His child by caring about His feelings.
16. I do not allow Satan to entice me by being aware of his tricks and depending on the Father for protection.
17. I demonstrate my Love for the Father by protecting Him from Satan – avoiding sin at all cost, with the Father's help.
18. I realize Satan hurt me by hurting my Father – God the Father.
19. I denounced the pomp and riches of this world.
20. I love poverty and asked God to grant me just enough to support life.
21. I threw the pomp and riches of this world at the face of Satan.
22. I try to emulate Jesus in everything – the Father is pleased – He grants Graces against Satan.
23. I feel concerned about the agony in the Sacred Heart of Jesus and share His agony with Him.
24. I aim at cheering His Most Sacred Heart up.
25. I am loyal to the Pope, the Vicar of Christ, Matt.16 vs. 14 – 19, Jn 21 vs. 15-17. Disloyalty to the Pope is disloyalty to Jesus.
26. I love and defend the One Holy Catholic and Apostolic Church founded by Jesus.
27. I promote loving God the Father with the heart and mind of a child.
28. I aim, like a child of the Father, to defend Him from His attackers as a child who loves his father would.
29. I mean everything I say to God. They come from the heart.
30. I aim at relieving the Father from the burden of seeking after strayed children by showing Him more love and winning souls for Him.
31. I allowed my love for God the Father to excel my love for my biological father as God is the Father of us all including my biological father – as I care about God's feelings, Satan flees. I am enjoying the Father's Love.

32. I regard the Blessed Virgin as my model.
33. I surrendered my will to God and trust in His Love for me like Mary.
34. I realize God does not compel anyone to do His Holy Will or to love Him. He gave everyone freewill because He is Love. Love is not for begging it is a thing of the heart.
35. I know He sought the Will of the Blessed Virgin Mary, she said "Yes" in the same manner I have said "Yes" to Him.
36. I surrendered my free-will to God and found peace and happiness.
37. I aim at winning souls to show devotion to Mary.
38. I have a personal relationship with Mary.
39. I love Mary more than I love my biological mother. She is the Mother of us all including my biological mother.
40. I am proud of my Heavenly parents and try to help them help me.
41. I have given to God a selfless love. I am not particular of what I will get from Him. I think of His happiness which is my priority.
42. I have complete trust in His Love for me.
43. I pray without ceasing.
44. I include Jesus in everything I do. I never take a step without Him.
45. I make Heaven my focus, not purgatory.
46. I aim at being a Saint.
47. I accept God's Holy Will for me whether I understand it or not.
48. I love the Holy Eucharist.
49. I aim at being always in a state of Grace by frequent reception of the sacrament of reconciliation.
50. I receive the sacrament of reconciliation every month and somtimes every forthnight.
51. I love Adoration of the Blessed Sacrament and I visit Jesus in the Tabernacle.
52. I have a very warm personal relationship with Jesus.
53. I have a very warm personal relationship with God the Father.

54. I am always myself before Him with respect and awe.
55. I have a very warm personal relationship with Mary, the Blessed Virgin, my Mum.
56. I pray for the Holy Spirit to always rule and direct my heart, to take care of my thoughts, words and deeds.
57. I thank God for being my Father, for creating me and loving me. I thank Him for all His benefits. For being my sweet All and All, unworthy though I am. I pray to resemble Jesus, to be completely one with Him, sharing with Him His suffering and His Joys. I ask Him to shine through me. I do not live for myself any more. I live for Jesus. I pray for God the Father to always be delighted when He looks at me by aiming at living according to His Precepts.

XIV. Conclusion

"Let us make man in our own image". What a wonderful loving statement from the Almighty God. When the full meaning of this beautiful statement dawned on me, I began to see God in everyone and admire Him in everyone because everyone reflects the beauty of God. I realized the creativeness, knowledge and wisdom of man came from the Almighty God, without whom man is absolutely nothing. He cannot exist without God. Man is functioning on borrowed wisdom, intellect, and creativity. Everything that man is, his capability, without mincing words, came from the Almighty God Who created him, loves him and endowed him with His nature which became stained with original sin to breed conceit. How wonderful and interesting it is to realize Human beings do not belong to their biological parents, rather they are meant to learn from their respective parents, here on earth, to know God, love and serve Him and finally return to Him Who is their real parent. All of humanity should be aware of this, as a guide, in whatever role one plays.

Before the fall of man, there was no need for man to learn to love God as man was already adorned with love for God. It is a man's place to adore, worship and praise God for all that He is, for His Greatness, to love and be obedient to Him. Failure to acknowledge the Supremacy of God spells unrest, lack of peace, disillusion, and unhappiness. Man is in the world to love, know and serve God and finally return to Him from whom he came. God is man's ultimate destination for eternal Joy. Having realized that God is my Father I gave Him all my love at once without hesitation, through His Grace. I loved my parents very much and gave them all my love as an obedient and loving daughter. Their feelings was always my priority as I had no intention of hurting them. The concern to please them by observing their rules won for me their love and affection. I became the darling daughter of my father and my mother. I was very close to them and always sought for their well-being. Now, I seek the well-being of God the Father Who loves me more than my parents, so much as to sacrifice His only begotten Son for me to reconcile me with Him, that I may have life and have it more abundantly, to have eternal happiness by Him in Heaven. Therefore, this world became a strange land, to me, an exile, lonely without my Heavenly Parents, Jesus and Mary, the holy Angels and Archangels, the Saints. I then determined to make Heaven at all cost because where my Parents are is my Home. My place is by God, my Father. The hope to be in Heaven some day with Jesus makes me dream of Heaven contemplating on Mum and me strolling down the streets of Heaven. What tremendous joy it gives me strengthening, and reminding me it is worth the trouble, to struggle for Heaven without counting the cost. The Grace of God is sufficient to sustain every sincere struggle.

Since children are given to parents to learn from them, through their relationship with one another, how to love God the Father, therefore, parents should love their children and cultivate in them an innocent selfless love and fear of God. Parents should live a God-fearing life, aiming at being good example for their children, realizing they are guardians and not owners, they belong to God, giving them good Catholic upbringing to enable them be rooted in the Catholic Faith. This makes them grow up into adulthood as true Christians. In so doing they would have raised up children with strong characters who would always, despite all the hazards of this exile have something to hold unto, the Faith from home. When the time is ripe, according to the Grace of God, then there would not be any hindrance to transfer this love for parents to God in a greater degree, thereby still retaining the love for their parents. Loving God begins at home.

Anthony knew the love I have for my parents was reserved for God, in a more beautiful degree, therefore, he was bent on damaging the image of my parents by creating false sinful stories with his evil prayers to influence me, trying to manipulate my mind. His inability to tarnish the image of my parents before me gave rise to his annoyance, accusing me of not being in love with him and not loving anybody in my life. According to him I was incapable of love. Well, how right he was by saying I did not fall in love with any one and how wrong he was by saying I was incapable of love. My heart could not open up to him because he was evil, besides, without his evil prayer "we brought you here" he would never have been able to manipulate me into his life. I thought the Angels of God brought me to him and who was I to oppose God's Will, but now I know the whole thing was a fallacious fallacy and had nothing to do with God.

My love was reserved for Jesus. I am not incapable of love. It was simply because my heart was not yet touched by any one. My heart was meant to love once and forever. It was waiting for Jesus the Prince of my heart and my life. When the time was ripe the Lord touched my heart and I fell head over heels in love with Him. He is my one and only Love. I love Him for better and for worse, in joy and in sorrow, in suffering and in pain, Jesus is mine, my Beloved. We suffer together and enjoy together because love is for sharing, love is suffering. My Jesus loves me and I love Him.

In everything around me I see God. I see Him in His creation and I simply love Him for being who He is – God! I love God the Father, God the Son and God the Holy Spirit. The Holy Trinity is my Love, how wonderful, how mysteriously beautiful and romantic is the love of God. How infinitely Merciful, how Kind, how Generous, how Good is the God Who created me and you. There is nothing I will not do for the God who made me and gave me His love. O how fortunate I am to behold the beauty of my Love in everything He created, the caress of His breath as the wind blows over me, The natural catastrophes, as they happen, send warnings of love, the desperation of unrequited love, sounding the urgency for the awareness of the living God, calling to mind the greatness and might of the Beloved. The sun with her beautiful rays, the smile of God, sends a touch of joy, the key of music into the heart filling it with her melody.

To a heart in love there is understanding and trust. All that happens to me and around me help me relate to God and that is what beautifies our relationship. For instance, when my one year old granddaughter refused me taking her into my arms as I lovingly reached out for her, not having seen her for a period of about two months, she had difficulties recognizing me, I was sad for her rejecting me. My whole thought and sympathy went out to Jesus realizing how sad He must be for the rejection of His children whom He loves so much and even gave His Life for love of them. Thinking of His Love, the Love of the Almighty Father, Who loves with the love of a mother, for His billions of children, I could not help but feeling sympathy for the great agony in his heart caused by His estranged children who deny Him their love. It is very painful when one is rejected by one's own.

When I remembered the instance when I could not lift myself up, having sunk down in dire pain to the floor crying, due to the pain coming from my hip bone, such a terrible pain, the pain of the bone is a very painful experience, it gave me an insight of what Jesus must have gone through carrying that heavy cross on the bones of His sacred shoulder. The heavy cross tore the flesh on His Shoulder, the flesh already weakened from the scourging, and exposed His bones. Anyone who has undergone bone surgery, broken leg or child labor, must have some knowledge of what I am trying to portray here, thinking of the labor pain which is a result of the baby resting on the pelvic bones. Jesus bore His heavy cross on His bare bones. What an agonizing pain He must have been subjected to not to mention the other types of pain coming from His different wounds all over His delicate Blessed Body. He endured these awful agonizing pains for love of man. What a terrible torture, considering His weakness. He lost much blood from the scourging and crowning with thorns, the soles of His feet full of wounds. It baffles me how He was able to walk with such soles carrying the heavy cross, uneasy in His whole Body, thirsty and hungry. He could not even ease Himself. Considering all Jesus went through for love of you what stops you from having pity on the God who loves you so much as to go through this torment, gave Himself in sacrifice for the love of His estranged children.

A pregnant woman, after she has given birth forgets the pain and rejoices over the birth of the new baby. Jesus has not been allowed to forget all that bitter passion He went through. We leave Him to continue suffering, banking on His infinite love for us and on His Divine Mercy. Do not forget God has feelings, did He not create us in His image? Therefore, do not allow Your Heavenly Father to go on suffering. Protect Him by surrendering yourself entirely to Him. Recognize Him as Your Beloved Father Who loves you and Whom you love. Show Him you love Him by keeping His Holy Will for your own happiness. God is always ready to welcome every estranged child of His, who turns to Him repentantly in humble trust. Keep your Heavenly Father happy He deserves it, stop sin and put Satan to shame he does not want your good. He makes you gamble with your life for his delight with you in hell, is that what you want?

My heart has a continual yearning for God the Father. I regard myself as His little girl in exile yearning to be united with my Beloved Father as soon as possible when I have accomplished His mission for me in this exile. The desire to defend the honor and interest of my Heavenly Father is most intense due to my helplessness to comprehend why such a Sweet Loving, Kind, and Generous God should suffer for His Goodness. Nevertheless, do not forget that this Good God, suffering and longing for your love is your Heavenly Father. Satan in his ingratitude, greed, selfishness and pride double-crossed the Most Merciful and Good Almighty God, your Father. All He requires from you is to love Him genuinely in return. To appreciate His Goodness, His generosity, keep His commandments, and render Him praise, worship and adoration. We must remember, that God, although all knowing, must create, love being His nature, had no choice but to grant every created being free-will because love does not compel.

Therefore, the question He must have known how Satan would react does not exist. Do not forget it is your Father Satan double-crossed. Would you sit back and do nothing? Satan wants to deprive you of your inheritance. It is your free-will to say "No" to Satan, turn your back at him by keeping the Heavenly Father's commandment and abide in His Love to ultimately receive your inheritance, the Glory that was yours from the beginning. Then you will swim in God's love, magnetized by His Beauty, drowned in admiration at His Majesty, loving Him and praising Him throughout eternity. To say "No" to Satan is to say "Yes" to life, to have life more abundantly. Be definitely assured, if you said "yes" to Satan you are in for perdition, to have death more abundantly in Hell. That is, being alive in death with Satan, eternal damnation with no escape. Would it not rather be wise to endure, with Jesus, any suffering you might encounter in this exile, offering it to His Holy Cross, trusting God with loving affection, patiently waiting, until you reach your eternal Home and be with the Father eternally? Therefore, denounce, with confidence in God, the pomp and riches of this world. It is Satan's weapon to entice you, and deprive you of your riches in Heaven. This does not mean wealth in itself is wrong, no, it all depends on how it is acquired and spent. If it be spent according to God's Holy Will then, there is nothing wrong with it. Try to please your Heavenly Father, He deserves it. He has sacrificed so much for you.

Take into consideration, how impossible it would be for you, if your children striped you naked in public, tied you to the pillar and scourged you, crowned you with a wreath of thorns, hit you on it with iron rods, slapped you and spat at you, on the face, and so on, finally nailed you naked, before a sea of people, on the cross, to forgive and love them. This would definitely be to you an abomination. I bet you would disown such children and regret you ever called them your children. If this would be the case, why do you then deny such a loving Father your love, Who forgave you, without grudges, despite causing Him all the above mentioned and more. He is the Almighty God, Lord of Heaven and Earth, Author and Giver of Life. He subjected Himself, with humility, to His bitter passion for love of you. Despite your sins, He is still protecting you, beckoning you to love Him and treat Him as Father. Satan manipulated the minds of God's children, made them extreme wicked, in his effort to weaken Jesus, at all cost, and make His saving mission a failure for him to possess the world he did not create, that does not belong to him.

Furthermore, consider the extreme sorrow in His Sacred Heart, as Jesus watched His own children torture Him. The children He so much infinitely loves, how He thirsted for their love and died of a broken heart. Satan, the embodiment of wickedness, the father of lies, as Jesus called him, in his desperate greed to own the world, thought he won the battle when the soldiers pierced the Sacred Side of Jesus with a lance, but got the surprise of his life when Jesus resurrected from the dead. It was then he knew he has lost the battle. Jesus resurrected triumphantly and conquered the powers of darkness. The Salvation which Jesus wrought for Humanity He paid with a bitter price. The whole human race owe Him everlasting "Thank You" Do not forget, today is the time, tomorrow may be too late. Although God is a very loving Father, any disobedient and stubborn child is a thorn in the flesh, to every parent, reason explains this, therefore, be aware God's patience with disobedience and stubbornness has limitation. He is a righteous Judge. Without Love we cannot reach God. Accept now His Divine Mercy and return love for love before He comes as a righteous Judge. He desires to see His reflection in us His children in order to enjoy His Fatherhood.

Being in love with God makes everything I do have meaning because I am every second with Jesus. My meals taste better while appreciating all He gives me. I sleep soundly in His Arms and wake up every morning to give thanks and praises to His Holy name. My worries become His, even when they are remembered they are not felt, due to the confidence, Jesus takes care of them in His own time. This knowledge makes my burden light and enhances my relationship with Him. Trust is always very necessary in a relationship. Besides, what is love without trust. Jesus is always faithful, He does not disappoint anyone who puts his trust in Him. The trouble is, can He trust us? are we faithful to Him the way He is to us? Do we spend a thought on Him to know about His feelings? How often do you tell Him "Father I love You" Try it, you can never say it enough, but please mean it and live it. There is nothing He has not done for His Children and is still doing for the salvation of all His children who would hear His voice and harken to it. He has given us His Most Sacred Heart, the furnace of Love, revealed to us through saint Margaret Mary Alacoque. His Divine Mercy chaplet, to prepare us for His second coming, through Saint Faustina.

This should strike a warning to the ears and make everyone eager to obtain Mercy from a very loving Father who would love to save all His children. A change of heart, turning a new leaf, repentance and earnest desire to please God is all that is needed to obtain God's Mercy. In the late nineties the Precious Blood chaplet and a set of other prayers have been Given to us by Jesus through Barnabas Nwoye, a Nigerian student during the Divine Mercy hour, prayers to safeguard us in this present time of the long awaited hours of darkness, the antichrist, evil spirits and their agents. Although the prayers of Barnabas Nwoye have not yet been recognized by the Holy See, they are authentic. it was after saying the Gethsemane prayers my name was written in the Lambs Book of Life and I received the tears of the Lord dropped into my eyes as mentioned before. At God's own time it would be recognized. Believe, have faith, open your heart to Jesus, be patient, be humble, rely on Him, leave the rest to Him. He knows what is good for you. Your needs are in the enclosure of His Heart, and He knows them better than you do, so make hay while the sun shines.

As a child of God, thanks to the Mercy of God, I have with Jesus and Mary a triangular relationship. The three of us really connected as in a real family relationship. This is how it should be with every one of us for we are all God's children, but we must first open our hearts for such a relationship. God, my Father, and the blessed Virgin Mary my Mum, both in Heaven loving me and watching over me, Their little girl, in this exile. Sometimes I long for my Heavenly Parents and desire my mission here on earth for my Heavenly Father would end soon to enable me be by Him and my loving Mum Mary in Heaven. I am very grateful to God for the Grace to console my blessed Mum and worry with her over Jesus my elder brother, as His little sister, friend, bride and daughter. It is a very wonderful sweet experience to be emotionally connected to Mum, the Blessed Virgin. Sometimes during the Hail Mary, we would weep together or in personal vocal prayer. Her tears would drop from my eyes and my heart would be moved. The Blessed Virgin is such a sweet loving tender caring darling Mum and I love Her very, very, very dearly.

O Holy Trinity, my God, I adore and love thee profoundly.
Sweet Beloved mine, Jesus King of my Heart, Lord of
my soul, Lover of my soul, Your tear Drops rolling down
my cheeks are pearls of delight, glistering like diamonds.
They send sweet sensations to my body and to my heart.

Also sweet melodies of love, in profound admiration for
You my God, my Love, they send. That Your Supreme Majesty tolerates,
me, who is less than half of an Ant, a nonentity overwhelms me. Your Juliet
You treasure tenderly in Your Sweet Most Sacred Heart,
the sweetest Heart that ever was, ever is and ever will be.

My heart is filled with songs of praise for You my wonderful
Beloved, sweet melodies only for a perfect Lover that
You are. I love You, my dearest Love, more than myself.
I trust in You like a baby in it's mother's arms, my Beloved.

How I long impatiently, my Romeo, for that beautiful day,
O Beloved mine, when the Father calls me Home to be
forever in Your Arms, O my sweet Lover, to live in You, with
You, forever in Your Heavenly Palace. O sweet joy Eternal!

On 25.11.2011 waking up from sleep, missing the Lord, I had such a deep longing for Him, although I consoled myself He had something in store for me, besides, His silence is love I should have patience, yet the longing was persistent. It was then I began to understand the dilemma of souls in purgatory not being able to see the Lord. How lonesome that must be, so close yet so far from the Beloved. Therefore, I asked the Lord to spare me such a horror by granting me the opportunity to work out my salvation here on earth so as to make Heaven. There is a great need to always be conscious, under all circumstances, that we are children of God destined for Glory.

O Blessed Trinity, my God, dearest Jesus, my sweet Beloved,
How dearly do I desire to be identified to Your Holy Cross, so
much so that suffering becomes sweet suffering for love of You,
Sweet Beloved of my heart. My place is beside You, my eternal Love.

My Divine Master, never do I want to be separated from my Love, not for a second. My heart desires to be intimately joined with my Sweet Beloved now and throughout eternity, always swimming in the ocean of His Love. My sweet Jesus, I love You more than myself and I accept with all my heart Your Holy Will for me – Amen.
The Lord's tears run down my cheeks.

It is sad observing the declined interest in religious or consecrated lives, the best path to choose on this exile. We are all on transit to a better world or to the worse. The God Who created us is shading holy tears for our blindness, our stubbornness in harkening to His calling for awareness of the enemy whose sole aim is to lead us to damnation, to a life far much worse than this exile without means of escape. Whereby, harkening to God's voice would lead to a far much better world, to everlasting happiness, everlasting life with God the Father, with the Holy Trinity. If only the priests would take their vocation more seriously, put flesh under subjection like St. Paul did, realizing the privilege to be Christ and not take the priesthood as a profession, show more reverence to God, especially while conducting mass, it would make a lot of difference as they are open letters to His Holy Catholic Church. It does not become a priest to convey the impression, lets get it done with, and that's it, as though the mass has become a routine lacking reverence.

Perhaps, it would be interesting to mention here God's Grace to me as I watched the mass on EWTN on 9.7.2012.

I witnessed with awe Jesus going down with the priest, father Joseph Mary Wolfe, who conducted the mass, as he knelt slowly before the consecrated Host. It was as though Jesus Himself was stooping down as He went down with the priest while His Face rested on the chest of the priest. I cannot describe it. It was awesome. Jesus wanted to show me He acts on His priests, therefore, Priests should aim at being holy for the love of the Holy God they represent. I have always admired the serenity of the priests on EWTN when they conduct the mass, especially during the liturgy of the Eucharist. They at least reverence God and portray the holiness of God. If only other priests would take example. I was also impressed most people receive Jesus in the mouth. That is the best way to receive our Lord and Master and not with the hand. The reception of Jesus with the hand seems to make him too common. Besides, as every particle is Jesus, with the hand one robs carelessly the particles on clothes or on the bench.

It is also possible the hand could be robed on the nose or on the tissue used in wiping the nose and so forth. Therefore, to make assurance doubly sure it is wise to receive Him in the mouth with respect and awe.

Only the priests' hands are consecrated to touch Him, not the laity. God is still the same, He has not changed. The early Christians received Him in the mouth or on the palm while they bent down to take Him with the tongue. There was much reverence and awe. The right hand was placed on top of the left hand and one bent down to take him with the tongue. Never was it heard that the Lord was taken from one laity to the other. There is no modernization with God for He does not change. One should not wonder why there is a decline in the consecrated life.

The modernization has succeeded in removing the awesomeness in the presence of the Almighty Father and the reverence He so much deserves. Today, He is ignored in the Tabernacles and left lonely. In His Divine Presence people sit talking and gossiping forgetting He is watching them. His love is taken for granted. „He loves us the way we are He does not mind if we chat", I get to hear. Yes, He does love us as we are, but not pleased when we give Him lip service. He expects love in return and love brings respect with it, therefore, if we loved Him from the heart we would realize He is a Holy God and Almighty. Therefore, it is only wise if we would recognize and cherish the humility of our Heavenly Father in reducing Himself to a Host, for our sake, for love of us, give Him reverence and sincere love in return. He is a long suffering God, a Most Merciful God, God of Love, but do not forget He is also a just Judge.

A Song
It is a thing most wonderful,
almost too wonderful to be,
That God's own Son should come from
Heaven and die to save a child like me.

And yet I know that it is true; He chose
a poor and humble lot, and wept and
toil'd, and mourn'd, and died for love
of those who loved Him not.

I cannot tell how He could love
A child so weak and full of sin;
His love must be most wonderful,
If He could die my love to win.

It is most wonderful to know
His love for me so free and sure;
But 'tis more wonderful to see
My love for Him so faint and poor.

And yet I want to love Thee Lord;
Oh, light the flame within my heart,
And I will love Thee more and more
Until I see Thee as Thou art.

The above sung reduced me to tears as I woke up with the melody in my heart early one morning. It catapulted my love for God to its highest peak. Perhaps it might have the same effect on you if only you could meditate on the words and allow the Holy Spirit touch your heart. If there was no danger the Son of God would not have subjected Himself to such an ordeal. Without His Love we are all dead. Now He has won life for us and He is waiting for us to reciprocate His love in order to have that life. Give Jesus a chance, forget worldly pleasures they lead to hell, get to know Him better and you will discover He is the best friend you can ever imagine, very reliable and faithful. Surrender your heart and will to Him and enjoy your Maker, Father, Beloved, friend and all and all. Give Him a chance for your own good, you will not regret. Be honest with Him and be yourself. Do not allow the perishable wealth of this world and the enticement of Satan deceive you. Remember, it is Heaven or hell, the ball is entirely on your court. As for me I have made my choice.

Oh, sweet Love Divine, my Beloved,
My poor little wretched heart Thou hast filled

with the sweet flavor of Your love, Oh,
Most Sacred Heart of my Love crucified.

My little heart Thou dost enthrone in the Most
Sacred Heart of her Maker. Thus one so low
And wretched, a nonentity, so unworthy enjoys,
like a princess, the Sweet Bliss of Love from her
Most Beloved, O sweet Love Divine, my God.

Intoxicated with Divine love my poor little heart,
endowed with Love so sweet, dare say, like the
Blessed Virgin, my mum, my soul magnifies
the Lord and my spirit rejoices in God my Savior.

He has regarded the lowliness of His handmaid,
for behold from henceforth I am the sweet beloved
of God, my Maker. O my Dearest Love, behold Your
handmaid, be it done unto me according to thy Will.

For You I live, in You I live, with You I suffer, for You
I die, for death in You, my dearest Love is but a ticket
to Heaven in Your sweet Arms, my delight in eternity,
O, how I look forward to it, my Eternal Love, so Divine.

I cannot help but feel it is God's Holy Will to use me for His purpose. For this reason I have asked Jesus to permit me fulfil this purpose, His purpose of creating me before He calls me Home. Otherwise Home is far much fulfilling and enriching where I would be forever in the Arms of my wonderful Beloved, magnetized in His Beauty, swimming in His Love, adoring and magnifying His Holy Name with all His Holy Angels and Saints throughout Eternity, where Joy reigns supreme, no sorrows, no pains and no death. Quite the contrary to this exile full of worries, tears, sorrows, envy, hatred and the like. I realized I am His Limbs, His

Mouth, in short I am Him for I no longer live my life but His. All that I am is Jesus. I am indeed head over heels in love with Him and I intend to remain in love with Him, now and in Eternity.

On September 12 I experienced God's love in a more deeper and special way. I found my soul so intimately united with Jesus in a very beautiful dimension beyond description. The soul knows itself as though one is a beautiful elevation in space, filled with warmth and thrills in God. It is a marvelous and wonderful feeling. Intimately united with God and out of this world, yet in it. Our God is a wonderful God. He is worth knowing. To be out of this world and yet in it only God can make it possible. It was a very profound tranquil experience for me. Words cannot describe it. One must experience it to be able to understand it. This is simply a slight glimpse to the beauty of God's Love which is for every soul that loves Him. It is indeed worth hoping for, therefore, be not blinded and deceived by Satan the evil seducer aiming at depriving you of God's Love and lead you to damnation. Hell is real and Heaven is Real.

> O my Eternal beautiful Love, Jesus Christ, my Lord,
> Redeemer and Savior, You Who have sacrificed so
> much for love of me, grant I beseech Thee, O my sweet
> agonized Love, that I may always be in a state of Grace
> in order to give you always a warm reception in my heart.
>
> O Eucharistic Food, nourishment of my soul. May my heart
> always be a Tabernacle of consolation for you. Make me
> worthy of Your love, may our relationship grow in perfection.
> Grant me a share in your agony O King of my heart, my
> Hope, my Life, my World, my Happiness, my Heaven – Amen.

– End –